MW00812810

Singing

An Extensive Handbook for All Singers And Their Teachers.

First eBook Edition Published 2016 by Novordium
Written by Ross Campbell

Concept, original design and formatting by Picador Design 2017
www.picadordesign.co.uk

This Hardback version ISBN number:
978-0-9955804-0-4

www.novordium.com

Ross Campbell

Websites
www.rosscampbell.biz
www.dailysingingtips.com

Twitter
@rosscampbelluk

Facebook
https://www.facebook.com/rossadcampbelluk

Ross is a graduate of the Royal College of Music in London and completed his studies on a scholarship to the Mozarteum in Salzburg. He won several awards whilst at the RCM and went on to sing in opera, oratorio and as a concert artist throughout the UK, France, Germany, Austria, Switzerland, Japan and South East Asia. He was also invited to create a number of roles in world premieres, particularly the Role of Saul/Paul in The Promise at London's Southbank Centre in 1997.

Ross was a founder member of The Kensington Consort and had a long association with the BBC, regularly singing on live radio broadcasts. He has recorded for Radio France as well as BBC TV.

He is currently Professor of Singing at the Royal Academy of Music in London, a post he has held since 1999, and was Head of Singing and Music at Guildford School of Acting at the University of Surrey until December 2011. Ross has students appearing in all West End Musicals and UK and International Tours on a continuous basis.

Whilst at GSA/University of Surrey, Ross created the internationally recognised MA degree course in the Practice of Voice & Singing (MA POVAS), and founded, built and launched the GSA Musical Theatre Examinations Syllabus in 2010, becoming the Director and Chief Examiner.

He was appointed to the ABRSM Panel of Mentors in 2001, and also the QAA Panel of Specialist Reviewers for Higher Education in 2003. He is regularly invited to assess at other Higher Education establishments in the UK, is invited to lecture on singing to both teachers and musicians throughout the UK, and has combined lecturing and performing on Seminars and Conferences in Beijing, Hong Kong, Malaysia, Singapore, Borneo and Malta.

Ross was invited to speak at the 'Music Education Forum' in Beijing in December 2010 and went on to launch a new Syllabus of Exams in Hong Kong and Macau at the same time, with accompanying masterclasses and workshops for both students and teachers. He was subsequently invited to deliver another paper to the same forum in December 2011 entitled "With One Voice - The Classical Sound & Musical Theatre Singing", and with accompanying workshops and masterclasses for Teachers.

Ross was commissioned by ABRSM to produce five anthologies of songs which serve Grades 1 to 5, for which he received the prestigious MIA award for 'Best Classical Publication 2009'. He also has extensive experience in designing courses, and producing documentation at Foundation, BA and MA degree levels.

His reputation and passion in sharing his own experience and research in professionally developing singing teachers and performers in musical theatre and commercial styles, often from classical backgrounds, has taken him to Beijing, Hong Kong, Macau, Singapore, Malaysia, Borneo, USA, Malta, Oslo, Stockholm, Zurich, Krakow, Dublin, Cork, Aberdeen, Belfast and numerous cities throughout the UK.

Ross created Musical Theatre Ireland (MTI) in 2012 based in Cork, offering specialist Musical Theatre training in singing, dance, acting and voice. He subsequently launched Musical Theatre UK (MTUK) in 2012 which is based in London.

Ross was invited to become a Consultant to Musical Theatre Poland (MTP) in 2013, travelling to Krakow regularly to conduct specialist singing training, workshops and masterclasses for MTP. He also became a consultant and patron to Aberdeen Academy of Performing Arts College in 2016.

CONTENTS

SECTION THREE - TRAINING THE SINGING VOICE

CHAPTER ONE
Relating Sound to the Anatomy

CHAPTER TWO
Relating Speech to Singing

CHAPTER THREE
Turning Speech into Singing

CHAPTER FOUR
What is Good Singing

CHAPTER FIVE
Practice

CHAPTER SIX
Suggested Warm-Up Routine

CHAPTER SEVEN
Further Training Exercises

SECTION FOUR - THE DEVELOPING VOICE

CHAPTER ONE
Babyhood to Adulthood... and Beyond!

CHAPTER TWO
The Classification of Voices

SECTION FIVE - PRACTICAL SINGING FOR ALL MUSICIANS

CHAPTER ONE
Singing is the Basis of all Musicianship

CHAPTER TWO
Aural Training - Using Your Ears to Find Your Voice

CHAPTER THREE
A Practical Approach to Aural Training

CHAPTER FOUR
Practical Singing for Examinations

SECTION SIX - MAKING MUSIC

CHAPTER ONE
Choosing Repertoire

CHAPTER TWO
Putting it all Together

SECTION SEVEN - PERFORMANCE

CHAPTER ONE
What Makes for a Successful Performance?

CHAPTER TWO
Preparing for Performance

CHAPTER THREE
Performing with Others

CHAPTER FOUR
Healthy Practices

SECTION EIGHT - THE PSYCHOLOGY OF SINGING

SECTION NINE - FURTHER DEVELOPMENT

SECTION TEN - TROUBLESHOOTING

CHAPTER ONE
Health Issues

Chapter Two
Recognising and Remedying Vocal Difficulties

GLOSSARY OF TERMS

APPENDIX I

APPENDIX II

Preface

We all know what a piano, a violin and a clarinet look like, and can quite easily understand how the basic mechanics of these instruments function, because we can see them and handle them.

Because we cannot see and handle the vocal instrument in the same way, its function can be somewhat of a mystery. Indeed, there have been autopsies conducted on great singers of the past in order to discover what made their voices so special. The results were inconclusive, because their larynxes looked no different from any other. The conclusion to draw from this is that it is the way the singer uses the vocal instrument which makes the singing voice special.

It is interesting to note that the laryngoscope, an instrument to observe the vocal folds in action, was developed not by a doctor, but by a teacher of singing, Manuel Garcia Jr (1805-1906). He wanted to understand why his father and his two sisters, Maria Malibran and Pauline Viardot, were such accomplished singers, whilst he, who had inherited the same vocal instrument, was not. His quest for this understanding made him one of the great teachers of singing history.

Instruments to observe the larynx have come a long way since the time of Manuel Garcia Jr. Optical fibre technology means that photographs and films can now be taken of the larynx in action, giving us a much clearer understanding of how it functions. The purpose of this book is to dispel some of the mystery for you, by defining the instrument, and explaining how to use this information for training voices.

Ross Campbell

Introduction

This book has been written for anybody who is interested in singing, particularly those who teach it. It also contains information which will be useful to instrumental teachers. It is designed to help all teachers to improve the aural and technical singing skills of their students, even if they are not first-study singers. Singing, after all, is at the heart of all aural work and musicianship.

There is much in this book to assist conductors of choral societies, music directors, and indeed anyone who works with singers, of whatever age and in whatever musical style. Moreover, singers who have progressed beyond a basic level will gain by using this book as a companion for their on-going development.

There is a simplified outline of the basics of singing in "The Fast Track" section. This will help you to become acquainted with the general principles which are treated in more detail in the other sections.

The book is structured so that the section "The Essential Anatomy" underpins those on "Training the Singing Voice", "Making Music" and "Performance". The nature of the anatomy section means that there is a lot of information presented, which could be difficult to assimilate all at once. Please think of it as a reference section, which can be either read all at once, or dipped into as required, so that the broader picture emerges over time.

"The Developing Voice" section is especially relevant for teachers training young adolescents through those years of marked vocal change. The "Making Music" section shows how to put the anatomy and training all together to prepare for a performance. This section also contains advice on choice of repertoire and how to build different styles of repertoire into the voice.

In the "Performance" and "The Psychology of Singing" sections you will find advice on the many small steps which lead to a successful performance, bringing motivation, healthy practice and personal fulfilment together to create a fuller picture.

General advice on understanding the root causes of vocal difficulties is given in the section on "Troubleshooting", along with some methods of resolving them. More detailed exercises to resolve difficulties are to be found in "Training the Singing Voice".

The broader issues of musicianship are covered in the section "Practical Singing for all Musicians", such as the role of examinations, aural training and the benefit of working in groups. The "Further Development" section offers advice on how to take singing into a more advanced field of study or performance.

Above all, the intention of this book is to present singing as a pleasurable activity, which, at its best, combines the physical, creative and emotional aspects of human expression.

Ross Campbell

SECTION ONE
The Fast Track

The Basics of Singing
Chapter One

This chapter will introduce you to the core principles necessary for singing. Very simply, these can be put into three categories:

Breathing

Making Sound

Modifying Sound

It is the working of all three in balance together which produces the singing voice. Knowing how they work is of great benefit to you in your teaching, and they are dealt with at length in ***The Essential Anatomy.*** Here we simply show them as part of the overall picture.

Breathing

Breathing is such a part of our everyday life that we can take it for granted and not think about how we do it.

When we breathe in, the lungs are filled with air because a muscle called the diaphragm contracts, causing the air to flow in. When we breathe out, the diaphragm relaxes and other muscles control the flow of exhaled air.

Because we sing on an exhaled breath, these muscles are very important in producing the singing voice. They give power to the voice and allow the singer control over the sound.

Making Sound

As with breathing, we often take making sound for granted, without thinking of how we do it or where it is coming from. Sound is made within the larynx, which is situated in the throat.

When we breathe out, air flows through the larynx and passes through a small space, which can open and shut. This opening and shutting action is caused by movement of the vocal folds.

When the vocal folds close together and air passes between them, they make the air vibrate, which our ears hear as sound. This action is similar for both speaking and singing.

The sound at this stage is basically a quacking noise. It then needs to be modified to produce the voice we are used to.

Modifying Sound

As with both of the above, it is so natural for us to modify sound that we do it without even thinking about it. The vibrating air, initially produced in the larynx, rises up the throat and into the mouth, resonating in both of these spaces. That is why the throat and mouth are called resonators.

Both the throat and mouth are capable of changing shape, and even the slightest change will modify the sound. We can see this very clearly in the difference between an "oo" vowel and an "ah" vowel.

The character of the sound can further be modified by the use of other resonators, such as the nose and other spaces in the head. The upper chest also acts as a resonator in much the same way as a "woofer" works in a hi-fi speaker.

Basic Guide to the Anatomy

Chapter Two

The following diagram shows the relative positions of all of the parts of the anatomy introduced above. This can be a point of reference for you for the more detailed information which you will find in ***The Essential Anatomy***. In these chapters, you will also find activities designed to help your students experience the physical side of singing.

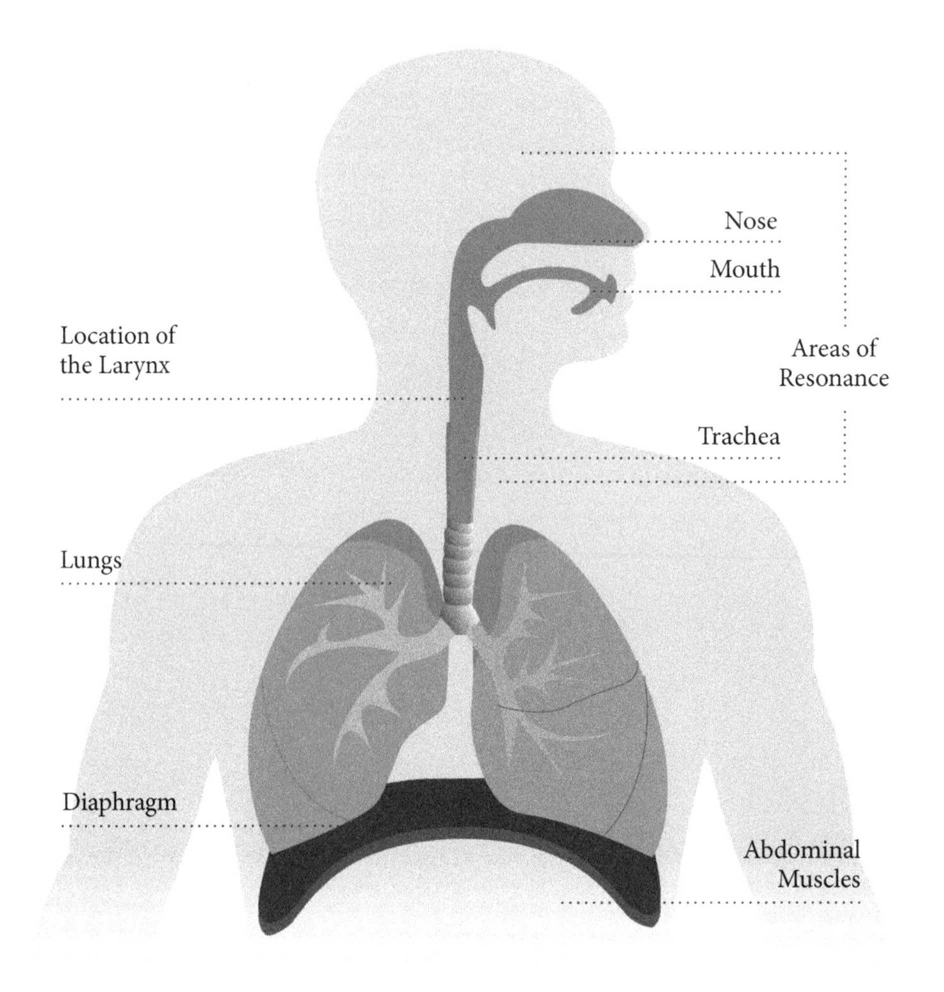

Diagram: Overall View of the Anatomy for Singing

Fig. 1. Overall View of the Anatomy; Image reference can be found on P. 222

The position of the larynx in the throat and air pressure in the chest work together for pitching notes. Increases and decreases in the air pressure also affect the volume (loudness and softness) of sound.

It is important when training the voice not to allow volume to increase as the pitch rises, because the higher notes will then become difficult to produce. The larynx will not be able to move properly in the throat if the air pressure is too great. The nature of this sound is often referred to as being "driven", or "over-blown".

The Basics of Teaching Singing

Chapter Three

Successful teaching lies in having a sense of what is relevant for each student, and knowing how to structure a lesson. However different the needs of each individual, there are core principles which should inform your teaching.

Greeting the Student

As obvious as this may seem, it needs to be mentioned here. The relationship between the teacher and student is fundamental to the success of the lesson. Putting your student at ease and establishing a good rapport begins with the small social niceties, such as "How are you today?" and "Have you had a good week?" Timid students will feel more confident to explore unknown territory if they feel at ease in your company.

Getting the Body Ready to Sing

The singing voice should not be turned on and off like a tap. Like other instruments, such as woodwind and brass, the instrument has to be warmed up in order to work well.

At the beginning of the lesson, gentle exercises focussing on the breathing mechanism, the larynx and the resonators prepare your student for the work ahead.

These exercises can be found at length in ***Training the Singing Voice***.

Posture

It is very important for the beginner to understand that the voice works best if the instrument – the body – is set up properly. There is an ideal physical set-up for the voice, which we call posture. Quite simply, posture addresses two areas, length of spine and breadth of upper chest.

The spine should be long, so no slouching! To achieve this, your student should be encouraged to think tall, with the back of the neck straight and the base of the spine tucked down. (Be sure that the knees don't lock!) This helps the breathing to function efficiently.

The breadth refers to the sense of widening in the upper chest as the shoulders move gently back. This helps to support the muscles in the neck.

A detailed activity for achieving good posture can be found in ***The Essential Anatomy***.

Breathing

A saying from the Italian Bel Canto School goes "If you know how to breathe, you know how to sing". Breathing is the foundation of good singing. If the air flow is controlled properly in the body, the throat will not be tempted to close and strangle the sound.

A good lesson will always address correct breathing as a means of supporting the voice. Again, the muscles which govern breathing should be warmed up, using increasingly vigorous exercises to build stamina and control.

Such exercises involve blocking the outward flow of air by the use of teeth, lips and tongue, so that the abdominal muscles have to work more intensively. An added bonus is that very little air pressure is placed upon the larynx by these exercises.

Activities which isolate and identify the muscle groups for breath control can be found in ***The Essential Anatomy***, and exercises for increasing stamina and control are included in ***Training the Singing Voice***.

Warming up the Larynx

The easiest and safest way to warm up the larynx is to use the sound "ng".

Stamina Building

Training a voice is also building a voice! The more efficiently the muscles can work, the better the singing will be. An athlete's performance improves through exercises which increase strength and flexibility.

For the same reasons, a singer needs to be given exercises to improve vocal stamina. This process cannot be rushed, and you should use exercises appropriate to the stage of development for each of your student.

There are many detailed exercises with a systematic structure in ***Training the Singing Voice***. These exercises can also be applied to sections of songs to increase strength, range and flexibility.

Sing Something Familiar

Build on your success! The next stage in a lesson could be for the student to sing a song which they know well, have just learned, or which they simply enjoy! This serves to reinforce a sense of progress and achievement, which will add to your student's growing confidence and prepare the ground for new repertoire.

Learning a New Song

You should always keep your student interested in their singing by introducing new repertoire at the appropriate time. A young singer can find note-bashing rather tedious, so limit the size of each new section to be learned to match your student's attention span.

Ending the Lesson

Time should always be left for the lesson to conclude rather than just stop! It is important that your student leaves each lesson with an idea of what they should be practising before they see you next. Depending upon the stage of development of your student, this could be a simple exercise or two, consolidating repertoire, preparing a new song, or even research.

The above suggestions for structuring a lesson are only a simple guideline to the basics. In your teaching, you will want to do far more than this, such as extending a student's range, developing the ability to sustain longer phrases, and to sing florid music accurately.

These issues, and many more, are addressed in ***Training the Singing Voice***, and solutions for common problems which you could encounter are to be found in the ***Troubleshooting section***.

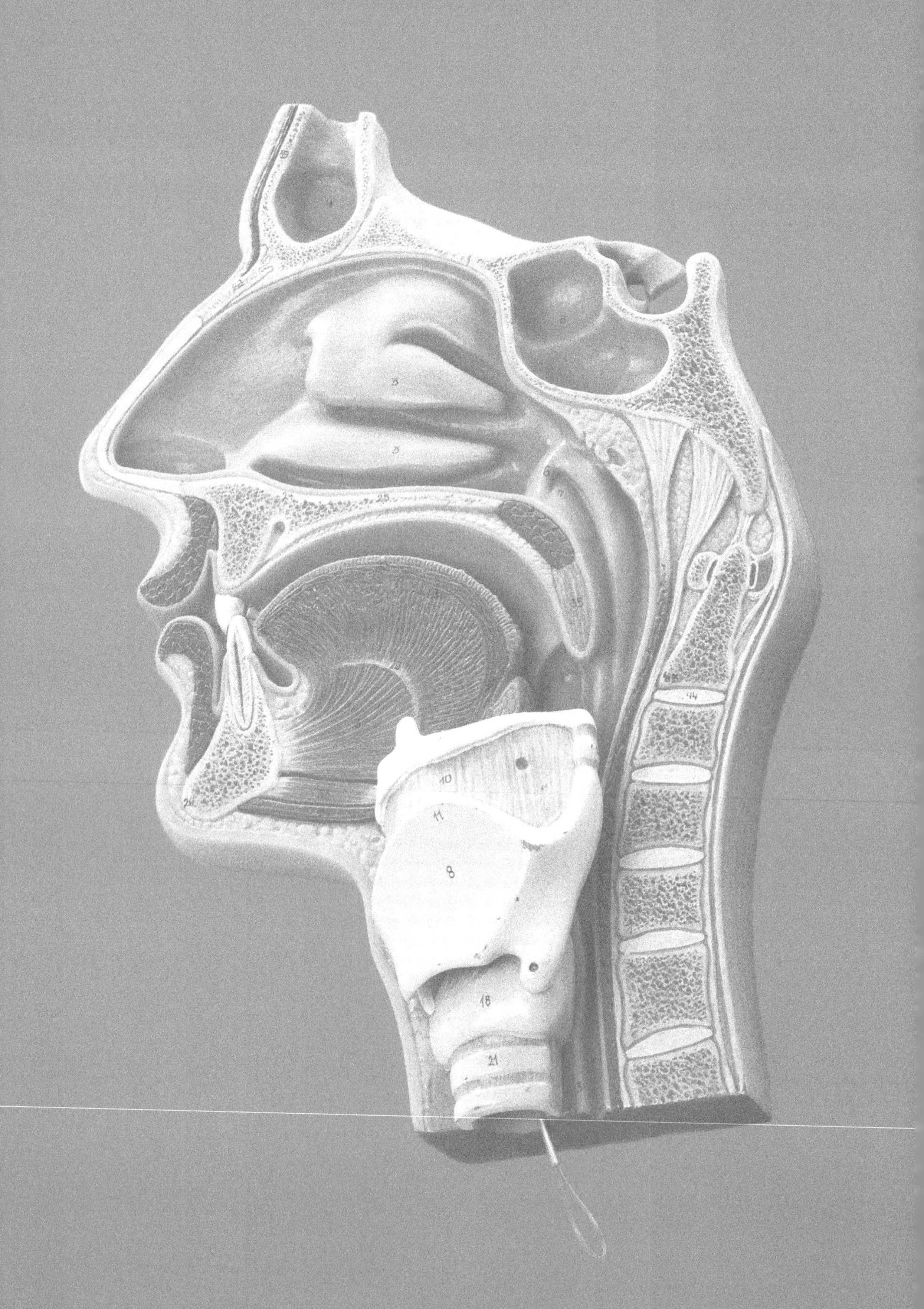

10
11
8
18
21
44

SECTION TWO
The Essential Anatomy

CHAPTER ONE
Singing is a Physical Activity

CHAPTER TWO
Breathing - Breath Support

CHAPTER THREE
Making Sound - The Larynx

CHAPTER FOUR
Modifying Sound - The Resonators

Singing is a Physical Activity

Chapter One

The Core Principles

This section will build upon what was introduced in ***"The Basics of Singing – The Fast Track".*** Singing is a physical activity involving the use of muscles. In order to sing well, the singer has to use the body in a particular way to make the voice function properly. The three core principles necessary for Singing relate to the following specific areas of the body.

Breathing - The Chest And The Abdomen
Making Sound - The Throat
Modifying Sound - The Resonators

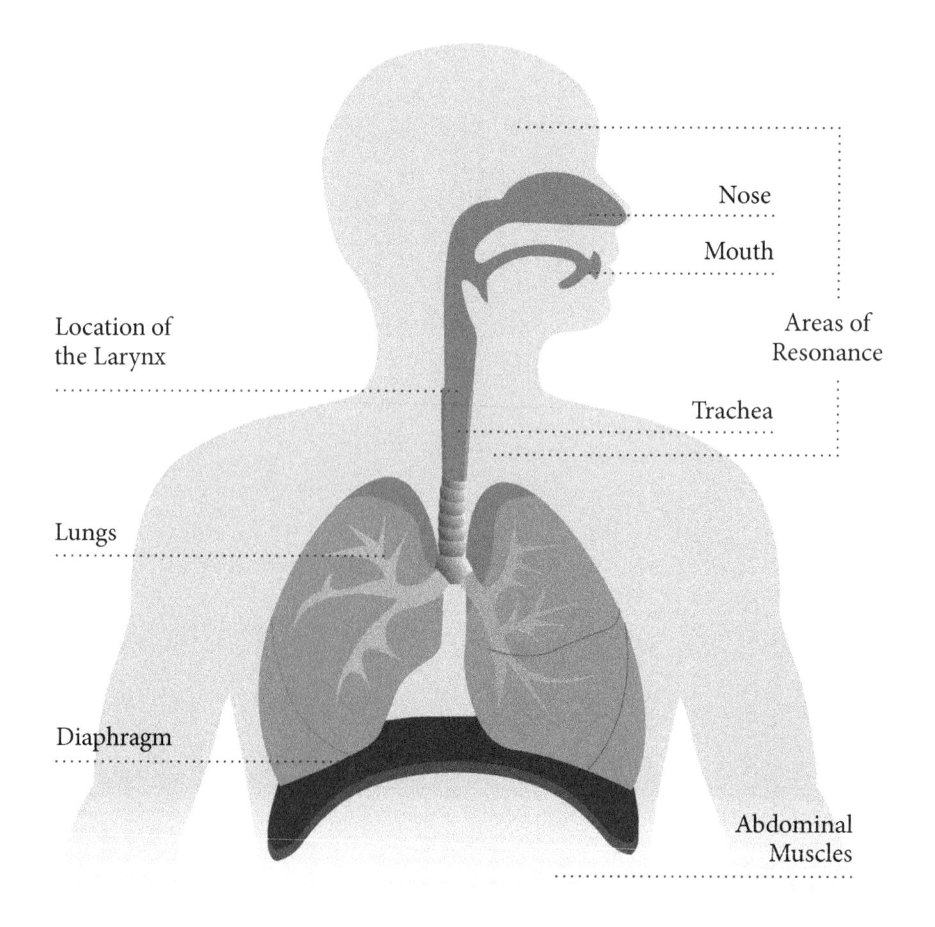

Diagram: Overall View of the Anatomy for Singing

Fig. 1. Overall View of the Anatomy; Image reference can be found on P. 222

The average listener can usually recognise whether a sound is "good" or "bad". You, the teacher, should also be able to identify how that sound is being produced, in order to train and develop the singing voice. You need to know how the body works when singing. A grasp of the general principles of anatomy should be a fundamental requirement in teaching. How expert you wish to become in this area is then up to you.

The Part Muscles Play

It is helpful to think of the singer as a vocal athlete. Just like an athlete, the muscles we need for singing have to function properly and be strong enough to meet the demands of the music. The act of singing involves muscular activity for breathing, making sound and modifying sound. Therefore, any teacher of singing should understand, at a basic level, how muscles work. You can then use this knowledge to train muscles to function properly, and to build up the necessary strength. We call this singing technique.

Basically, muscles do three things:

1. they contract
2. they relax
3. they can be stretched

In singing, all three actions can be happening at the same time.

Contraction of a muscle is often called flexing a muscle. When a muscle contracts, it shortens and the muscle bulges. This can be easily observed by looking at the bicep in the upper arm – even a child knows how to flex this muscle! Muscles contract through use of energy, a word which you will see used many times in this book. Energy is vital to singing.

When muscles relax, they go back to their original length and the bulge disappears.

The most basic muscular action is the spasm (jerk reflex); it is a quick contraction of the muscle. So, short, intensive activities followed by periods of rest are much more productive than sustained, heavy work, especially for young people. There must be a rest and recovery period.

Muscles enjoy being stretched. Athletes do stretching exercises to loosen up the body and to warm up. The easiest stretch for a singer is the siren, which is dealt with in the section ***Training the Singing Voice, Chapter 6, Suggested Warm-up Routine, Sirening.***

Muscles rarely work in isolation; they tend to work in groups. Knowing which muscles should be doing which action is all part of the training. However, when energy is misapplied, muscle groups may work in opposition to each other. This conflict of muscular energies we refer to as tension. Energy is a friend to singing, tension is an enemy.

The importance of the above can be seen just by looking at the tongue. It is not just one muscle, but a combination of several, working together to comprise the fastest moving organ in the body. It is a very flexible organ, and allows the singer to alter the shape of the mouth and pharynx with speed and precision. If there is a conflict of energies in the muscles of the tongue, it can result in tongue-root tension. This has a very negative effect on the singing voice. The function of the tongue and exercises to control it in singing will be dealt with in the section ***Training the Singing Voice, Chapter 4, What is Good Singing? The Voice Sounds Clear, The Tongue; Tension in the Jaw and Tongue.***

Muscle Memory and Training

Muscles "remember" the actions they perform. The more often these actions are repeated, the more efficient the muscles become at doing them. The clearest example of muscle memory is your accent. This is the result of years of repetition of particular muscular actions of the tongue and throat. It is habitual – you don't have to think about it! If you want to change your accent, you have to create new muscular habits!

Training a voice involves building up muscle memory which allows the voice to work at its best. A singer may arrive for their first lesson with muscles which are under-active, over-active or used incorrectly. Breaking down old habits and creating new ones which are more efficient is an essential part of teaching singing.

In your teaching you should encourage regular practice and rehearsal, because it is by repetition that the new muscle memory is established. Repetition also builds stamina for more prolonged and sustained singing. The result will be that your student will learn how to sing with a wider range of pitch and dynamics, and remain vocally fresh.

Posture

As has already been stated in the section ***The Basics of Singing - The Fast Track***, it is very important for the singer to understand that the voice works best if the instrument – the body – is set up properly. There is an ideal physical set-up for the voice, which we call posture. Quite simply, posture addresses two areas, length of spine and breadth of upper chest. The relationship of these two is called ***alignment***.

The spine should be long, so no slouching! To achieve this, your student should be encouraged to think tall, with the back of the neck straight and the base of the spine tucked down. (Be sure that the knees don't lock!) Breathing can then function efficiently. The breadth refers to the sense of widening in the upper chest as the shoulders move gently back. This helps to support the muscles in the neck and stabilises the ***larynx***.

It is necessary to state at this point that the breath cannot work properly if the body is not correctly aligned, for example if collapsed in the centre. The larynx can't work easily if the chin juts forward.

The two main elements of good posture and proper alignment are:

the long spine
breadth across the upper chest.

Activity:
LONG SPINE
Stand with your feet slightly apart to find a comfortable balance. The base of the spine should be gently tilted downwards, and the nape of the neck should stretch backwards into a gentle C curve. The spine is now lengthened.

BREADTH ACROSS THE UPPER CHEST.
Clasp your hands behind your back and then gently pull the shoulders back by lowering the hands. There will be a feeling of stretch in the pectoral muscles as the chest widens. Release the arms while maintaining this posture.

Students should always be encouraged to be aware of their own posture. Good posture may feel unnatural at first because of incorrect use of muscles, for example slouching, but the student should persevere until it becomes habitual.

Breathing - Breath Support
Chapter Two

The Breath Support System
Control of breath underpins all speaking and singing. Air is taken into the lungs either through the mouth or nose as you breathe in, and passes out of the body as you breath out. On its way out, it passes through the larynx and is used to power the voice. The following are the most important parts of the anatomy controlling the use of breath in voice production.

the lungs
the diaphragm
the abdominal muscles
related muscle groups

The Lungs
These are large sacs lying within the rib cage, above the diaphragm. Their main purpose is to provide the body with oxygen which they extract from the inhaled air. The air left over is then exhaled, and we can use it to make sound. They cannot inflate or deflate by themselves because they have no muscles of their own. They inflate and deflate due to the action of the ***diaphragm.***

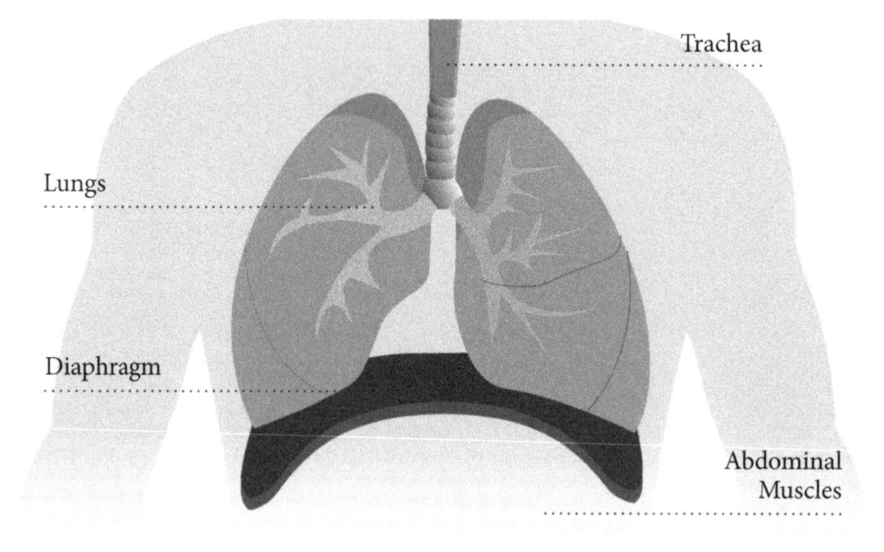

Fig. 1. Overall View of the Anatomy; Image reference can be found on P. 222

The Diaphragm

This is a sheet of muscle attached to the lower edges of the rib cage and to the spine at the back. When relaxed, it lies in a dome shape underneath the deflated lungs. When it contracts and moves downward towards the abdomen, we are breathing in. The lungs inflate as we inhale. It is important to note here that the diaphragm is contracting as we breathe in, and relaxing upwards back to its original position as we breathe out.

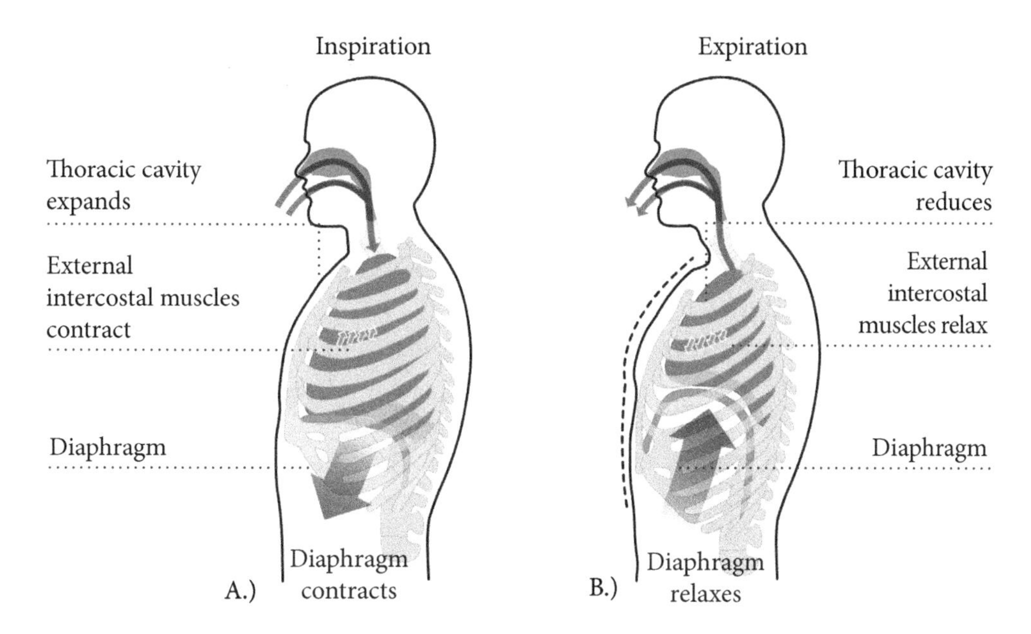

The Action of the Diaphragm

Fig. 2 The Action of the Diaphragm; Image reference can be found on P. 222

[Diagram A: The Action of the Diaphragm - contracted]
When the diaphragm contracts, it moves downwards. Air is inhaled and the lungs inflate as this happens.

[Diagram B: The Action of the Diaphragm - relaxed]
When there is little breath in the lungs, the diaphragm is relaxed and sits high in the rib cage.

The diaphragm's main work is to bring the air in! The vocal folds vibrate as we breathe out. Since the diaphragm is becoming more relaxed as it returns to its original position, we cannot depend on the diaphragm to support the voice. Other muscle groups have to be used in order to control the outward flow of air. It is these muscles which support the breath and give power to the voice. Locking or holding the diaphragm interferes with the way these muscles work and impedes the free flow of air. This is tension.

The Abdominal Muscles

These muscles are easy to observe in action. They are situated above and below the navel in the front of the torso. When they contract, they assist the process of breathing, particularly supporting the outward flow of breath. The work of the abdominal muscles is particularly important for long phrases, whether spoken or sung. Contraction of these muscles should not interfere with the diaphragm as it relaxes.

Activity:

1. Using the fingertips, find the band of muscle above the navel and just below the sternum.
2. Push the fingertips into this band of muscle to feel how elastic it is.
3. Make a long and vigorous "V" sound with the upper teeth on the lower lip, and observe how this muscle contracts, pushing the fingertips outward.
4. Repeat this exercise with the band of muscle below the navel.

This is the same muscular action used in supporting the breath for singing. Please note that the navel is not being pushed outwards as these muscles contract. To identify this, place a fingertip in the navel and make a long "SHHH" sound. The navel naturally moves inwards towards the spine as the air is exhaled.

Related Muscle Groups

The abdominal muscles are helped in their work by muscles in the back, the sides and the pelvic floor. Some of these are not as easy to observe in action as thc abdominals, but nevertheless they play a vital role in controlling the use of breath in both speaking and singing.

The action of these muscles can be observed by using a similar exercise as above. For each of these activities, the student should create a blockage of the airflow by making a lengthened "V" or "SHH" sound, in order to make the muscles contract.

Activity:

1. For the back, place the palm of the hand on the back muscles just below the ribcage. Make a "SHH" sound and feel the muscles contract.
2. For the sides, place both hands just below the ribcage on either side of the body, the fingers in front and the thumbs to the back. Make a "SHH" sound. Squeeze gently as the sound is made, and the contraction of the muscles is easily observed.
3. For the pelvic floor muscles, sit upright on a hard chair. Make a "SHH" sound. As the sound is made, there will be a very slight uplift of the torso as the muscles contract against the chair.

Making Sound - The Larynx

Chapter Three

Location of the Larynx

The larynx is commonly referred to as the Adam's Apple or Voice Box. It sits in the throat on top of the wind-pipe ***(trachea)***, below the root of the tongue. The root of the tongue is attached to the hyoid bone, which is one of the first bones to be formed in the foetus. The hyoid bone is the only floating bone in the body as it is not attached to any other bone. The larynx is attached to the hyoid bone and suspended below it. The hyoid bone gives the larynx a wide degree of flexibility.

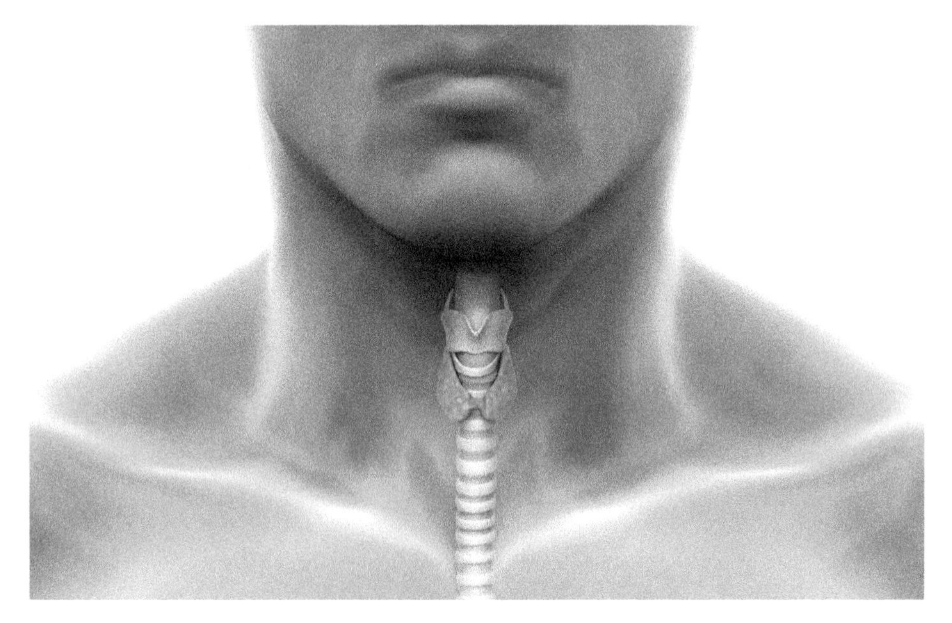

Diagram: The Location of the Larynx

Fig. 3. The Location of the Larynx; Image reference can be found on P. 222

The larynx is a valve constrictor whose primary function is to close the air passage when swallowing food and drink, preventing us from choking. It also closes very firmly to trap air in the chest (thorax) when high levels of effort are required, such as lifting a heavy weight. The larynx is also our organ for speaking and singing – this is where the sound originates.

The larynx is generally larger in men than in women, and therefore can be more easily seen in men. It moves up and down in the throat – just watch a man swallow to see it in action. This movement has important consequences for singing.

Activity:
You may observe the movement of the larynx by looking in a mirror and swallowing. The larynx initially moves up, and then moves down again.

To feel the movement of the larynx, place a finger on the Adam's Apple and swallow. The action is very apparent.

It is important that the singer is aware of this movement, as it plays such a major role in pitching and voice quality.

Component Parts of the Larynx
The larynx has several parts, all of which are capable of independent movement, but which usually work together for singing. The main ones are:

the thyroid cartilage
the arytenoid cartilages
the cricoid cartilage
the true vocal folds
the false vocal folds

These are held in place by a system of muscles, tendons and ligaments, sometimes called the vocal scaffolding. The larynx moves up and down in the throat because of the action of the scaffolding muscles acting as a form of support. You will read more about how this affects the sound in ***Voice Qualities*** later in this section, and in the section on ***Training the Singing Voice, Chapter 1, Relating Sound to the Anatomy, Voice Qualities; Chapter 4, What Is Good Singing, The Voice Sounds Clear)***

Cartilage is a strong, stretchy fibrous tissue which provides support to the skeleton. Cartilage can be soft, as in the ear lobe, or firm, as in the larynx.

The Thyroid Cartilage

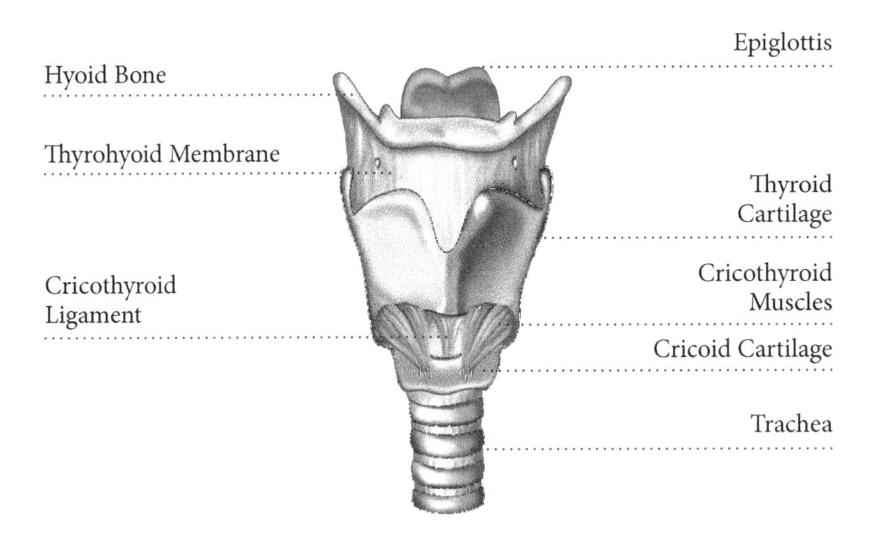

Diagram of the larynx as seen from the front

Fig. 4. The larynx as seen from the front; Image reference can be found on P. 222

This is the largest component of the larynx, forming a shield which houses and protects the vocal folds. It is the most obvious part of the Adam's Apple, and is easy to locate. It can move independently of the other cartilages by tilting forward. This movement gently stretches the true vocal folds, lengthening them, whilst at the same time changing the angle of the folds in relation to the airflow which is coming from directly below.

The following diagrams show the change from horizontal to angle of the true vocal folds in relation to air flow. It is essential to master this movement, called thyroid tilt, as it helps in attaining higher pitches.

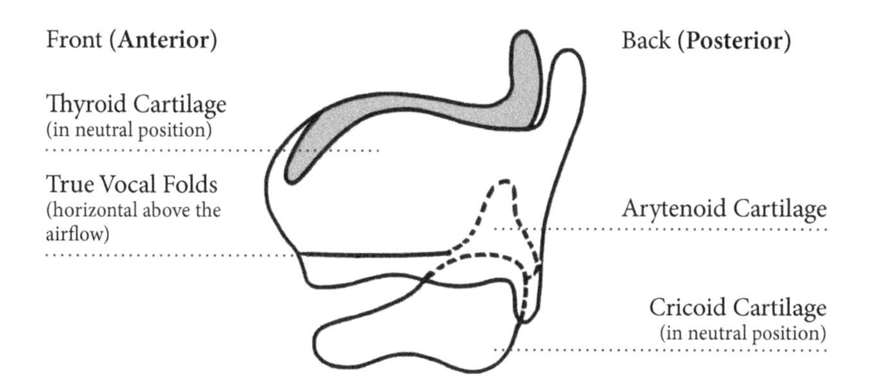

Diagram: Thyroid Cartilage in Neutral Position

Larynx seen from side, showing thyroid cartilage in neutral position (speech quality)

Fig. 5. Thyroid Cartilage In Neutral Position; Image reference can be found on P. 223

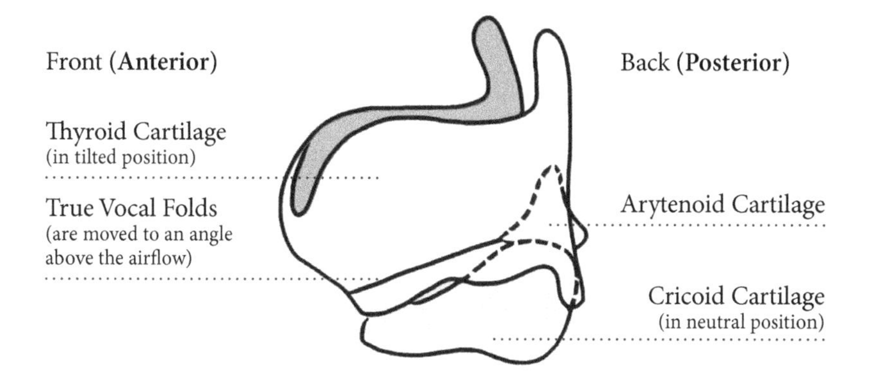

[Diagram: Thyroid Cartilage in Tilted Position]

Larynx seen from side showing thyroid cartilage in tilted position (sob/tilt and cry/tilt qualities)

Fig. 6. Thyroid Cartilage In Tilted Position; Image reference can be found on P. 223

Activity:

1. Place a finger on the Adam's Apple. Think of a puppy whimpering.
2. Make a crying, whimpering sound at several different levels of pitch. The movement of the thyroid cartilage will be very small, but it is essential that you observe a forward tilting movement.
3. Repeat these actions silently to reinforce the feeling of this movement.

This activity is difficult to observe in a mirror as it is so slight, but it is very important to gain control of this tilting action.

The Arytenoid Cartilages

These pyramid-shaped structures are situated at the back (posterior) end of the vocal folds, sitting on the shelf of the cricoid cartilage. There are two of them, one for each vocal fold.

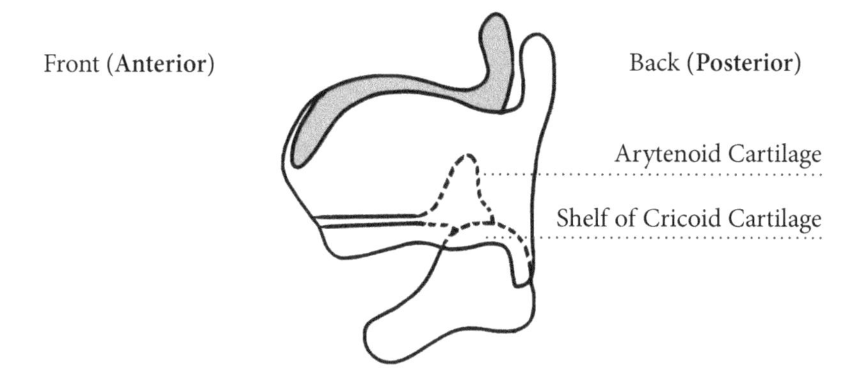

[Diagram: The Larynx Seen from the Side, Showing One Arytenoid Cartilage Sitting on the Shelf of the Cricoid Cartilage.]

Fig. 7 The Larynx seen from the side; Image reference can be found on P. 223

The arytenoid cartilages can move in several directions. They move outwards to open the ***glottis*** (the space between the vocal folds, through which air passes). This is called abduction of the true vocal folds. They move inwards to bring the vocal folds together, thus closing the glottis and creating the correct position for sound to be made. This is called adduction of the true vocal folds.

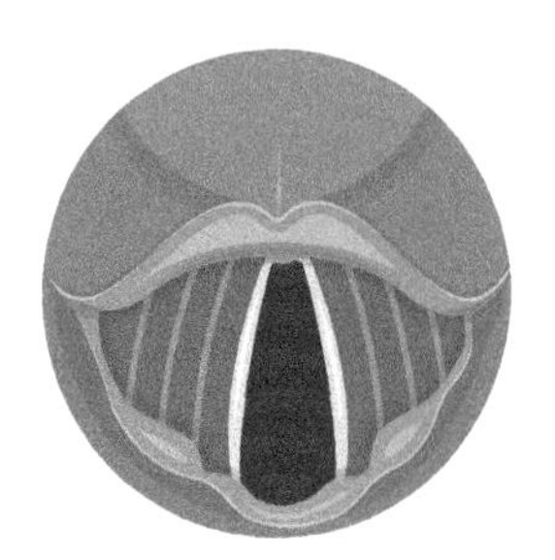

Vocal Folds ABDUCTED In Order to Breathe

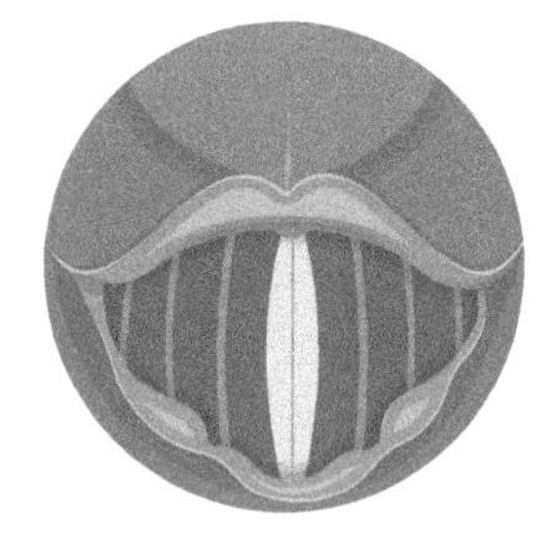

Vocal Folds ADDUCTED In Order to Speak

[Diagram: The Arytenoid Cartilages Opening And Closing The Glottis]

Larynx seen from above, showing the arytenoids opening and closing the glottis

Fig. 8. The Arytenoid Cartilages; Image reference can be found on P. 222

Activity:

1. Smile broadly. Take the width of the smile down into the throat; this will help to open the vocal folds widely.
2. Breathe in and out through the mouth with no sound at all. When you can do this, the folds are fully open. This exercise helps gain control over moving the arytenoid cartilages into the open-glottis position.
3. Cough gently, almost silently! At the start (onset) of this sound, the vocal folds are fully closed. The gust of air of the cough gently blows them apart.
4. Repeat the start of the sound without the cough (completely silently). If you are doing this correctly, you will find that you are holding your breath, because the vocal folds are fully closed.

Practising this silently gains firmer control of the closing action of the arytenoids, which, in turn, helps to solve the problems of breathiness in singing.

The arytenoid cartilages can also flip backwards, which raises the back (posterior) end of the true vocal folds, stretching and stiffening them. Stiffening the true vocal folds means that they cannot contract easily. In this position, the only way to get volume is by blowing more air. When sound accompanies the arytenoid flip it is recognised as a yodel, as the voice changes quality into falsetto. There is a clunking action accompanying the sound, as in a gear change!

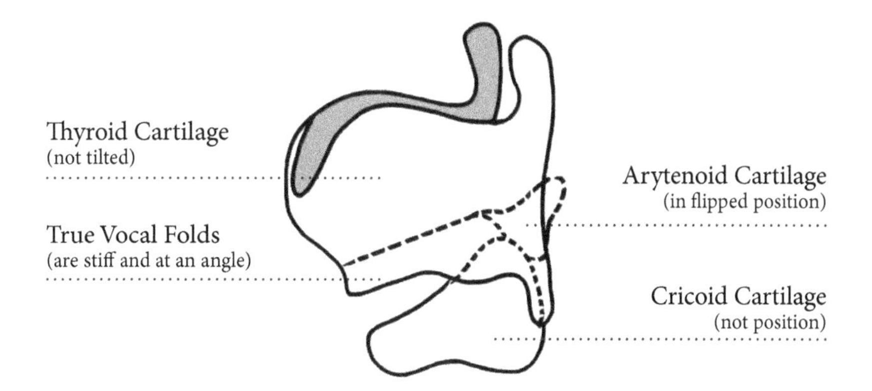

[Diagram: Falsetto Quality]

Larynx seen from side, showing arytenoid flip (falsetto quality)

Fig. 9. Falsetto Quality; Image reference can be found on P. 223

Activity:

1. Blow air in a "hoo" sound on a middle note for your voice range, quite loudly.
2. Falsetto works best at higher pitches, so raise the pitch of the note. This time blow softly, in order to avoid going into full voice.
3. When you can comfortably make the sound on a high pitch, go back to the middle range and move back and forth between the upper and lower pitches. There will be a clunking feel and sound as the arytenoids flip back and forth.

This is a perfectly natural function of the voice, and will not damage it in any way. It is important that you can feel when the arytenoids are in the "flipped" falsetto position (do it silently). This action is common to all voices. It's not only men who yodel – think of Maria singing about the Lonely Goatherd in "The Sound of Music".

The Cricoid Cartilage

This part of the larynx is completely circular, like a ring. It sits below the thyroid cartilage, and is much smaller in size. The back (posterior) section of the cricoid is higher than the front, and the arytenoid cartilages sit on this little shelf. When the cricoid is tilted, the back rises and moves towards the front (anterior) wall of the thyroid cartilage. This action means that the true vocal folds are shortened and thickened. It happens quite naturally in a yell; children employ this mechanism regularly (especially in the school playground), and babies put it to very effective use to gain attention. Because the true vocal folds are thickened, the muscular energy is high and the volume is loud.

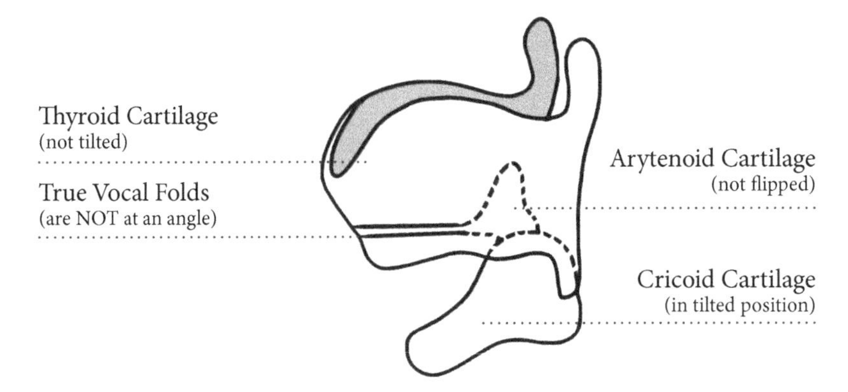

[Diagram: Belt Quality]

Larynx seen from side, showing cricoid cartilage in tilt (Belt quality).

Fig. 10. Belt Quality; Image reference can be found on P. 223

We would not recommend teaching cricoid tilt in singing for children and young adolescents. The high level of energy within the larynx demanded by this mode of singing requires a degree of stamina which would not yet be in place for this age group. It will be dealt with in the later sections on ***Training the Singing Voice, Chapter 1, Relating Sound to the Anatomy, Voice Qualities, and The Developing Voice, Chapter 1.***

The True Vocal Folds

Sound comes from the vibration of air caused by the opening and closing of the true vocal folds. These are sometimes referred to as the vocal cords.

When air passes over the true vocal folds as they are brought together ***(adducted)***, they open and close rapidly, causing the air to vibrate. If they were fully closed, no air would be able to pass and there would be no sound. When viewed on camera at normal speed, they appear to be fully closed; however, when viewed in slow motion, it can be seen that they are opening and closing in a cycle, chopping the air into little puffs. For example, when singing concert pitch "A", they are vibrating at 440 cycles per second. If they vibrate slower, the pitch lowers; if they vibrate faster, the pitch rises.

The true vocal folds are muscular, and can be contracted just like any other muscle in the body. Contraction of this muscle tissue causes thickening of the vocal fold mass ***(thick folds)***, which will affect the sound produced, making it louder and fuller. An increase in air pressure also stimulates contraction of the muscles within the vocal folds. This can change the pitch and/or increase the volume.

The true vocal folds can also be stretched by movement of the arytenoid cartilages and the tilting of the thyroid cartilage. Movement of these cartilage systems lengthens and thins the folds ***(thin folds)***, which enables easier access to the higher notes. The length of the true vocal folds has a direct affect on pitch. In general, the shorter the folds, the lower the note and the longer the folds, the higher the note.

The true vocal folds are usually larger for the lower voices and smaller for the higher voices. However, in all cases they are much smaller than we would imagine, given the amount of volume that they can produce. When they are closed, the area covered is not much bigger than a little finger nail!
This diagram, looking down the throat from above, shows the white band of the vocal ligament running down the edge of each fold in a ^ shape. You cannot see the muscular part of the folds in this photograph, because they lie

underneath the pink tissue of the false vocal folds – more about these later in this section.

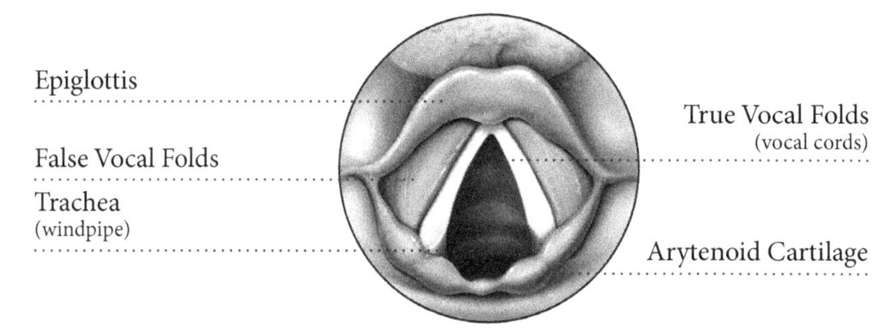

[Diagram of The Vocal Folds as Seen from Above]

Fig. 11 Diagram of the Vocal Folds as seen from Above; Image reference can be found on P. 222

The diagram shows the vocal folds in breathing mode, (they are apart, allowing air to go in and out of the lungs). The top section of the ^ is at the front of the throat (anterior), where the vocal folds are permanently joined and attached to the thyroid cartilage.

The lower part of the diagram shows the back (posterior) ends of the vocal folds attached to the arytenoid cartilages, of which there are two – one for each vocal fold. When these cartilages are moved apart, they cause the folds to move apart, thus opening the glottis (the space between the folds) and allowing air to pass. Because the folds shown here are apart, there would be no vibration, and therefore no sound.

When the arytenoid cartilages move towards each other, they bring the vocal folds together. This is called adduction. Air passing over the folds in this position causes them to vibrate. Sound is produced. If the vocal folds are not properly brought together (adducted), the sound will be breathy.

The False Vocal Folds

These are bands of tissue which lie above the true vocal folds and which reinforce the closure of the glottis. They can interfere with (constrict) the proper vibration of the true vocal folds by pressing down on them. The false vocal folds need to be kept apart (retracted) to prevent this undesirable action from happening

Nervousness, some emotions and high energy levels can all trigger the false vocal folds to close, causing constriction. A conscious effort must be made to prevent this natural tendency, and to keep them out of the way when speaking and singing. A variety of problems can arise when the false vocal folds are not properly retracted. These issues will be addressed in the sections on ***Training the Singing Voice, Chapter 4 What Is Good Singing, The Voice Sounds Free and Troubleshooting, Chapter 1 Hoarseness and Chapter 2 Constriction.***

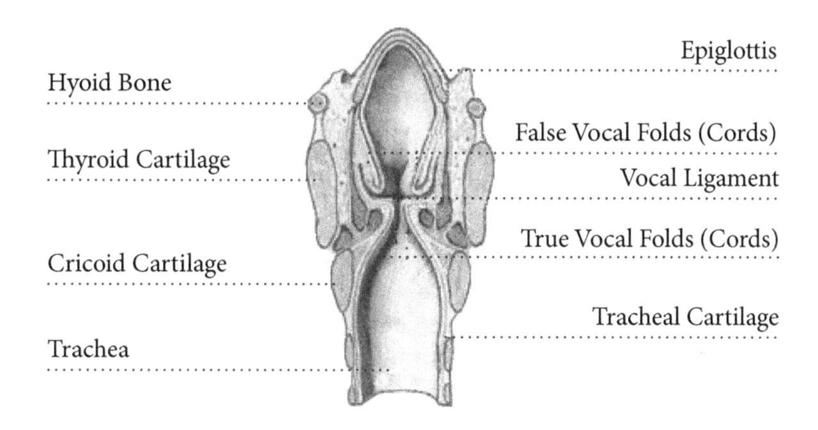

[Diagram: The False Vocal Folds]
Larynx seen from back (posterior view), showing the position of the false vocal folds in relation to the true vocal folds
Fig. 12 The False Vocal Folds; Image reference can be found on P. 222

The false vocal folds naturally retract during laughing and sobbing. Laughing is more fun, so use this to practise retraction; the feeling in the throat is one of width.

Activity:

1. Laugh silently. Notice the sense of width in the throat. It is very useful to practice this silently, because you can focus on the muscular work involved without the distraction of sound.

The more vigorous the silent laugh, the stronger the muscular activity. Learning through the feel of an activity rather than by the sound produced will help you gain better control over the mechanisms involved.

Voice Qualities

At this point it is necessary to explain the concept of voice quality. This term refers to the different types of sound which we can make, and which are directly related to movements of each of the component parts of the larynx, as previously explained.

Voice researchers generally agree that a voice quality is determined by:

1. the position of the larynx in the throat (high or low)
2. how the moving parts of the larynx relate to each other (tilt, flip)
3. a learned component, such as the native spoken language, regional accent and any input from vocal training.

The basic voice qualities for singing are:

speech
cry/tilt
sob/tilt
belt
falsetto

The following diagrams show the relative positions of the thyroid, cricoid and arytenoid cartilages and their effect upon the vocal folds in order to create the voice qualities.

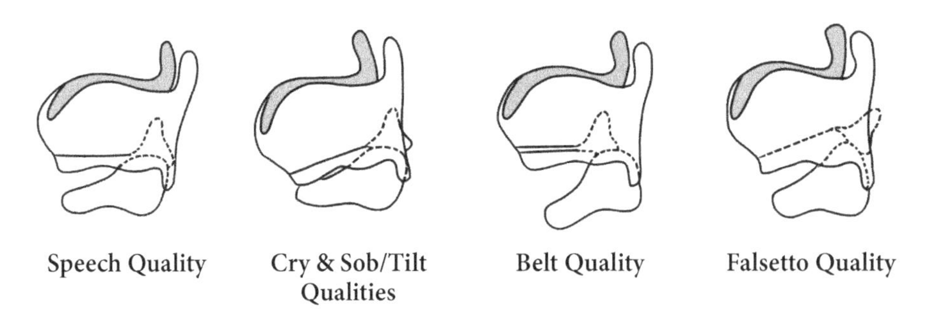

[Diagram: Laryngeal Postures for Voice Qualities]

Fig. 13 Laryngeal Postures for Voice Qualities; Image reference can be found on P. 223

In ***speech quality***, the vocal folds are in a horizontal position above the air flow; the thyroid and cricoid cartilages are not tilted. The larynx is in the mid-point of the throat. This is the neutral position.

In ***cry/tilt quality***, the thyroid cartilage tilts forward, gently stretching the vocal folds and positioning them at an angle above the air flow. The larynx is in a higher position within the throat, relative to the neutral position of speech quality.

In ***sob/tilt*** quality, the thyroid cartilage tilts forward, gently stretching the vocal folds and positioning them at an angle above the air flow. The larynx is in a lower position within the throat, relative to the neutral position of speech quality.

In ***belt quality,*** the cricoid cartilage tilts downward at the front, moving the rear shelf forwards. The vocal folds are shortened and thickened (compressed) by this action. The larynx is high in the throat, relative to the neutral position of speech quality.

In ***falsetto quality,*** the arytenoid cartilages are flipped back. This raises the vocal folds at the back, so that they are at an angle to the airflow. This action also stiffens them, so that the muscles in the vocal folds cannot contract. The sound is breathy, and is stronger at higher pitches. It becomes very weak at low pitches. The larynx can be high or low in the throat and the thyroid cartilage may be tilted or not.

Modifying Sound – The Resonators

Chapter Four

Vocal Tone

The tone of a note (whether it sounds bright or dark, sweet or harsh, rounded or thin) is created by the resonators. The initial sound made by the vocal folds is little more than a quack. It now needs help to become the beautiful sound we recognise as singing. It is the resonators which allow the singer to do this.

If we consider some instruments of the woodwind section of an orchestra, we can see how changing the shape of the resonating space modifies the sound. The piccolo, which is short and very thin, sounds high and brilliant. The alto flute is longer and wider, has a bigger range and a richer tone. The base flute is the longest and widest of the three, plays lower notes and has a deep mellow tone. In a similar way, the singer can change the length and width of resonating spaces and so create a broad spectrum of tonal colour.

The singer can feel where certain frequencies resonate in the body. Higher frequencies (cycles per second) have a shorter wavelength and are felt to resonate in the smaller cavities such as the nasal and head sinuses. Lower frequencies have a longer wavelength and appear to be resonating in the larger cavity of the chest, while the cavities of the mouth and oro-pharynx serve the middle range of frequencies. It helps if you think of the tweeter, woofer and mid-range cones of hi-fi speakers, which perform a similar function.

Good singing demands control of the resonators to produce the tone required, whether this be a beautiful sound or not! This can be acquired through training.

The Resonators
The resonators are:

the throat (pharynx)
the mouth
the nose and head sinuses
the chest
the aryepiglottic sphincter (twang)

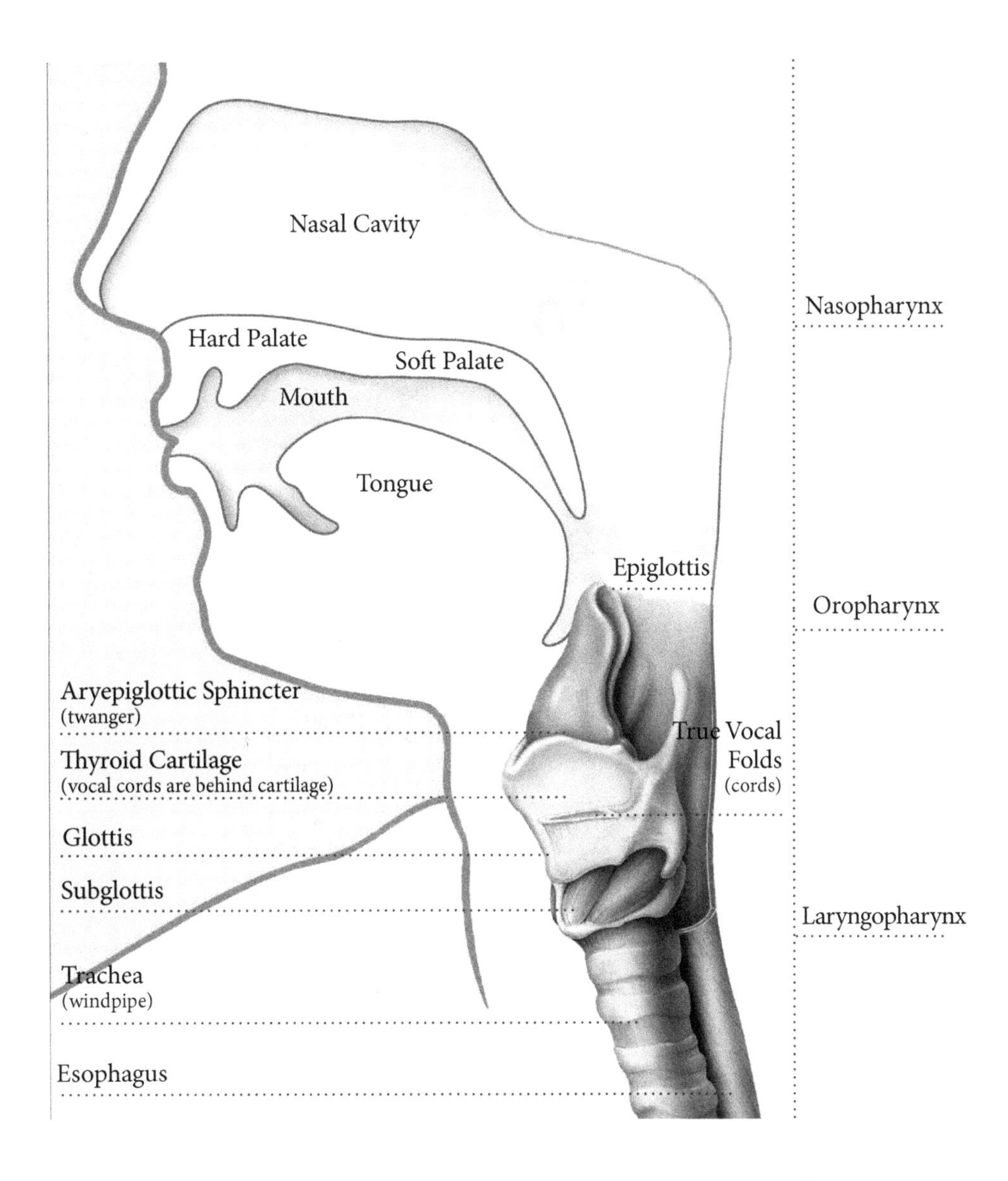

[Diagram: The Resonators in the Head and Neck]
Fig. 14 The Resonators in the Head and Neck; Image reference can be found on P. 223

The Throat (Pharynx)

The tube-like space extending above the vocal folds is called the pharynx, commonly known as the throat. The air in this space vibrates because of the opening and closing action of the vocal folds.

There are three sections to the pharynx:
1. The space in the throat directly above the vocal folds is called the laryngo- (or hypo-) pharynx; this is the lowest part of the pharynx.
2. The space in the throat at the back of the mouth is called the oro-pharynx; this is the middle part of the pharynx.
3. The space in the upper throat behind the nose is called the naso-pharynx; this is the top of the pharynx.

The tube of the pharynx can be lengthened or shortened by raising or lowering the larynx. The pharynx can be widened by contracting muscles in the neck. These changes to the shape of the pharynx have a similar effect upon vocal tone just as with the woodwind instruments mentioned earlier.

The rise and fall of the larynx also has a direct affect on the pitch of a note. This will be explored in the section on ***Training the Singing Voice, Chapter 1, Relating Sound top the Anatomy, Pitch.***

Activity 1:
1. Place one finger on the thyroid cartilage (Adam's Apple). Swallow, and feel the movement of the larynx as it rises and then falls.
2. Repeat this exercise, except that this time, keep the larynx in the high position – do not allow it drop by completing the swallow. Then say "Heee".
3. Again, repeat the exercise, this time allowing the larynx to fall to its lower position by completing the swallow. Again say "Heee" with the larynx in this low position.

There will be a noticeable difference in the nature of the sound. You may also use a mirror to observe the action of the thyroid cartilage if you wish.

Activity 2:
1. Place the hand gently around the lower neck and then give a gasp of surprise. The muscles of the neck will be felt to contract, widening the throat.
2. Repeat this exercise SILENTLY. This helps in gaining voluntary control over the width of the laryngo-pharynx.

The Mouth

The mouth works in conjunction with the oro-pharnx as a resonating space. The oro-pharynx is the middle section of the throat at the back of the mouth. The width of the oro-pharynx has a direct effect on the nature of the sound produced by adding harmonics (overtones) to the sound.

Activity 1:

1. Place the hand gently around the upper neck and then give a gasp of surprise. The muscles of the neck will be felt to contract, widening the throat.
2. Repeat this exercise SILENTLY. This helps in gaining voluntary control over the width of the oro-pharynx.

Vowels are formed by changing the shape of the mouth and middle throat (oro-pharynx), in conjunction with movement of the tongue and lips. The tongue is not a resonator, but plays an important role in oral resonance. It must not be allowed to block the oro-pharynx by moving backwards, as it does with the yawn mechanism.

Activity 2:

1. Place the hand gently around the middle neck. Say the vowel "Eee" followed by the vowel "Ooo". Notice that the tongue changes position in the mouth, the lips move as the vowel changes, the larynx moves in the throat.
2. Repeat this exercise silently. You can feel the vowel change even without the sound.

You may observe in a mirror the lips changing position and the movement of the larynx if you wish.

The Nose and Head Sinuses

The nose and head sinuses are important and easily recognised resonators.

The nose is a large resonating space. There is a big difference between nasal resonance and singing in the nose. Nasal resonance is often referred to as "forward placement" or "singing in the mask". It is an additional vibration to the oro-pharynx and mouth. Singing in the nose is a sound used in some country and western singing and for characterisation in song, such as the Wicked Witch in a pantomime. It may also be used in Musical Theatre for characterisation. It is not recognised as good singing for most music, however it is quite safe.

Singing in the nose means that the nasal vibration dominates. This interferes with the clarity of diction and muffles the sound. Singing in the nose is caused by the soft palate being in a low position, so that the sound travels up the throat and into the nose. This can be avoided by raising the soft palate, which partially closes the doorway into the nose and deflects the sound into the mouth.

Activity:

1. Without holding your nose, gently blow the nose. This action lowers the soft palate, as the air will blow through the nasal cavities to clear them.
2. With the soft palate held in this position, say "Heee". The sound will be nasal, resonating strongly in the nasal cavities.
3. Gently hold the nose so that the nostrils are blocked. Again say a very nasal "Heee". You will feel the nose vibrating.
4. Repeat the sound so that the nose does NOT vibrate. The sound will be resonating in the mouth more than the nose, because the soft palate has lifted.
5. Release the hold on the nose and repeat the "Heee" without nasality.
6. To recognise the feeling of the movement of the soft palate, repeat this exercise until you can produce the "Heee" sound with and without nasality and without pinching the nostrils.

The head sinuses are small spaces which enhance the higher frequencies of the harmonics of a tone, sometimes called overtones. The higher voices, such as sopranos and mezzo-sopranos, clearly feel the resonating activity of these sinuses like a little buzz in the head. The lower voices may not feel these resonators as clearly as the higher voices, but it is important for them to become aware of these sensations. The naso-pharynx works in conjunction with the head sinuses and is most effective with the soft palate in a raised position. When these resonators are working well, it is often referred to as "high placement". The tone may sound flat and under pitched without the higher frequencies produced by the head sinuses and naso-pharynx.

The Chest

The chest acts as a secondary resonator, and is responsive to lower pitches and a lower larynx. What is often referred to as a "chest" voice arises from the sensations of resonance in the chest cavity and lower throat, in response to lower pitches and thicker true vocal folds. It is not a separate "voice" at all.

Activity:
Place the palm of the hand on the sternum (at the centre of the upper chest). Make a low-pitched, vocalised sigh "Haaa".

There will be a feeling of vibration through the hand coming from the chest, when the larynx and pitch of the sound are low.

The action of all of the resonators can be felt in the following activity.

Activity:
Starting on the highest pitch of your range, gently hum an "MMM" sound and slide down to the lowest pitch of your range.

You will feel the resonators working from the head sinuses down to the chest as the pitch lowers. You will also feel the lips vibrate strongly as the sound resonates in the mouth and oro-pharynx.

Twang and the Aryepiglottic Sphincter

Twang is present in many languages and accents, and is a safe way of using the voice. It can be clearly heard in the American and Australian accents, and in the Chinese languages. Twang acts as a natural amplifying system for the voice, with the added benefit of requiring less muscular energy from the true vocal folds. Twang can be used in all voice qualities and is a resonating device which makes the voice brighter and more intense. It is also very useful for accessing the higher notes of the range as it thins the vocal folds and makes the transition from lower to higher notes easier.

Twang is produced by the contraction of the aryepiglottic sphincter. A sphincter is a ring muscle; when it contracts, the ring gets smaller. The aryepiglottic sphincter muscle runs around the outer edge of the epiglottis. The epiglottis sits above the larynx and is attached to the root of the tongue. It acts as a type of lid closing over the wind-pipe (trachea) during the act of swallowing. When speaking and singing, the epiglottis is lifted out of the way, but the aryepiglottic sphincter can still be contracted. This contraction creates a small resonating chamber in the pharynx just above the vocal folds.

Twang is the sound which children make naturally when taunting each other in the school playground.

Activity:

1. Say "Nyeh, nyeh, nyeh, nyeh, nyeh!" like a child being nasty to another child!

You can be very nasal, as this is the easiest way of accessing this sound.

2. Say "Yeh Yeh Yeh!" in the same way, but with the soft palate raised. This shows that twang need not be nasal.

Conclusion

To sum up, this is how the singing voice functions:

the sound is produced in the larynx
the sound is powered by breath from the lungs
the flow of breath must be sustained by the breath support system
the breath support system and the larynx work together and are inter-dependent
movements of the larynx and its component parts change the quality of the voice
the sound is further modified by the resonators

An important concept which should guide you is that the larynx, where the sound is produced, is a valve constrictor: its primary function, in other words, is to shut down. It can do this so efficiently as to be air-tight, as in the act of swallowing. In swallowing, the larynx shuts down to ensure that whatever is swallowed does not go down the wind-pipe (trachaea). Any constriction or shutting down is counter-productive, because singing requires the larynx to be free.

It is important to maintain the freedom of the larynx so that it can function as a singing instrument. Nerves and worry can also trigger the shutting-down reflex of the larynx. If it tries to shut down during the act of singing, the voice will sound squeezed and constricted. Further, more serious, problems may arise from this. The control of airflow must be the job of the breath support system. When properly supported, the voice will emerge freely and under control.

You should be able to recognise what physical activity is happening in order to produce the sound you hear. The accompanying activities in this section are designed to help you locate and use each anatomical part described. Muscles have memory, and your body understands a lot more than your mind may give it credit for, so repeating these activities helps your body as well as your mind to understand how it functions.

All of these anatomical mechanisms work together to create the singing voice, but they can be trained in isolation, as the activities in this section have shown. Gaining control over each mechanism is vital to gaining complete control of the singing voice. We will deal with this further in the section on ***Training the Singing Voice.***

There is a lot of technical information in this chapter – but be assured! You don't have to understand it all at once. Use this chapter as a constant source of reference, until the workings of the essential anatomy become second nature.

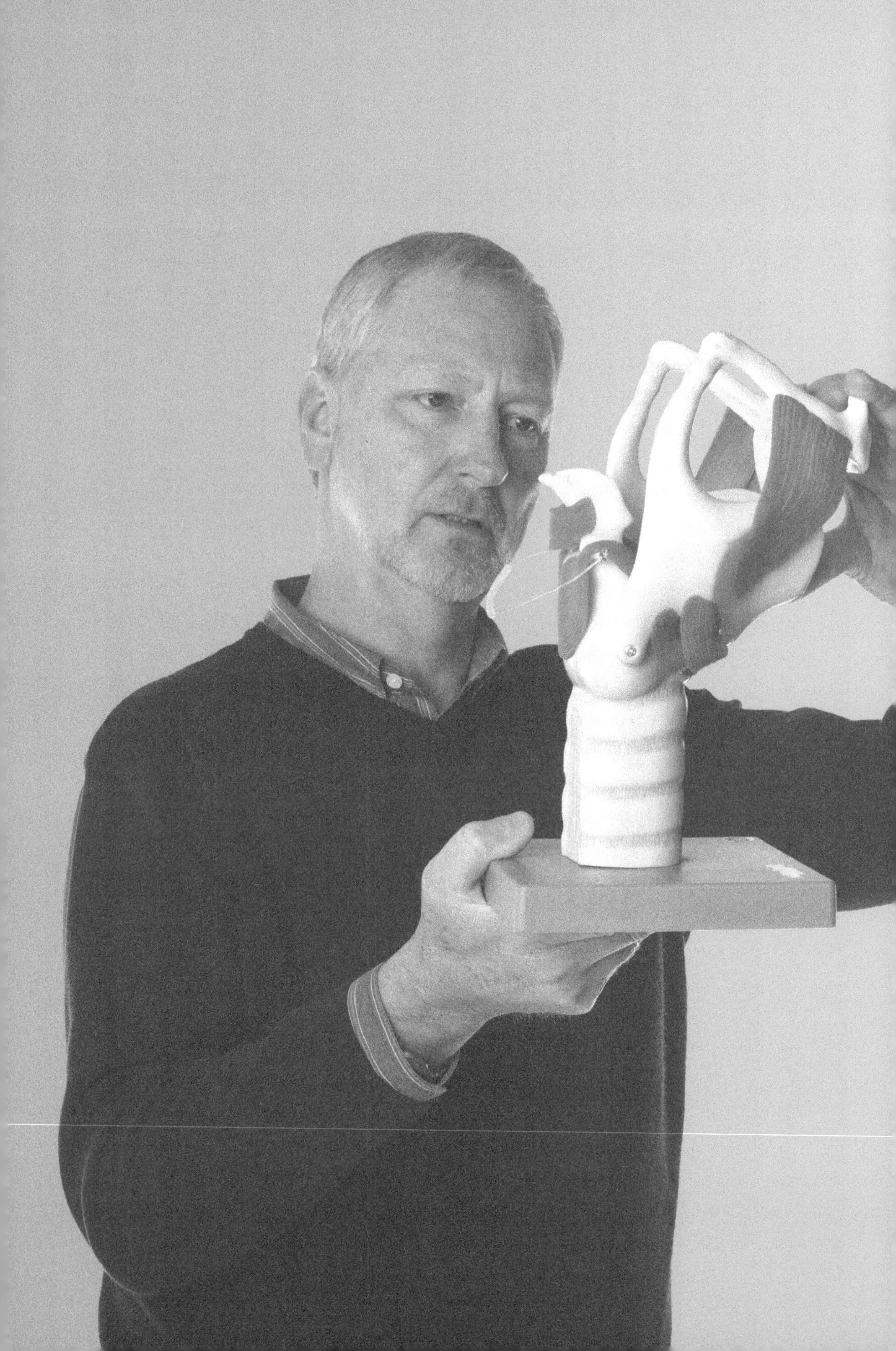

SECTION THREE

Training the Singing Voice

Relating Sound to the Anatomy

Chapter One

Proper training of the Singing Voice requires that the teacher know the mechanisms which create sound, and understand how they function, both independently and in relation to one another.

An essential of good teaching is the ability to recognise, by sound alone, which of the mechanisms are working and how they are working. Without this skill, training the singing voice is effectively limited to trial and error.

This analytical ear is the greatest tool the teacher of singing can possess, and will ensure the continuing vocal health and development of the singer's voice. Many of the practical activities and exercises contained in this section work equally well with groups as with individual singers.

The exercises outlined and explained in this section should be used in conjunction with the expanding song repertoire from the outset. Phrases within songs will often throw up problems which these exercises can resolve. It is important to balance the technical work of the exercises with the creativity of singing and building of repertoire in any one lesson.

Pitch

As a general rule, the pitch of a note relates to the anatomy in two ways:

1. the position of the larynx in the throat
2. air pressure in the thorax

You can see the larynx rising in the throat as the pitch rises on a siren, and lowering as the pitch lowers. So a general rule to be drawn from this is that the larynx is higher in the throat on high notes and lower on low notes. If a singer has trouble attaining high notes, it may be that the larynx is not sufficiently high.

If you put your hands on your sides just below the rib cage and make a "VVV" sound, you will notice that the muscles contract. When you go from a lower pitch to a higher one on the "VVV" sound, you will notice that the muscles contract even more. This is because the higher notes require greater air pressure, which is created by the firmer contraction of the breath support muscles. So the other general rule is that the higher notes require greater air pressure. If a singer has trouble attaining high notes, it may be that there is not sufficient air pressure. The breath support system is not working hard enough.

However, air pressure is not only related to pitch. It also relates to volume. The position of the larynx in the throat and air pressure work together in very close association for pitching notes. Increases and decreases in the air pressure also affect the volume (loudness and softness) of sound. It is important when training the voice not to allow volume to increase as the pitch rises, because the higher notes will then become difficult to produce. The larynx will not be able to move properly in the throat if the air pressure is too great. The nature of this sound is often referred to as being "driven", or "over-blown". ***(See The Fast Track, Chapter 2 Basic guide to the Anatomy)***

Volume

Generally speaking, an increase in volume is achieved by an increase of air pressure. The increase in air pressure thickens the true vocal folds ***(thick folds).***

When we contract the abdominal muscles of the Breath Support System there is an increase in air pressure. ***(See The Essential Anatomy, Chapter 2, Breathing - Breath Support)*** The energy level in the body becomes high, resulting in increased volume. Even louder sounds can be achieved when twang is combined with the increased air pressure. ***(See The Essential Anatomy, Chapter 4, Modifying the Sound, Twang and the Aryepiglottic Sphincter; and twang is also dealt with later in this chapter)***

When less volume is required, the air pressure is reduced. This causes the true vocal folds to vibrate only at the very edges, which is called thin folds, as the full muscular mass of the true vocal folds is not required. Of course, even in piano singing, the higher notes require a relative increase in air pressure, and therefore the muscles of the breath support system must be engaged. In such instances of piano singing, the use of twang aids projection of the voice without increasing the volume.

The exercise of messa di voce (literally "placing of the voice"), which was much practised in the bel canto tradition, is actually the transition from thin to thick folds, and back again, on one sustained pitch. This requires a the singer to have refined control over the breathing support system in order to be able to create the air pressure necessary to trigger the thinning and the thickening of the true vocal folds without changing the pitch or timbre of the sound.

Voice Qualities

We will mention voice qualities often in this section, so it is good to repeat what they are. You should be able to recognise which voice qualities are being used and with what degree of success. The mechanics of the voice qualities have already been outlined in ***The Essential Anatomy, Chapter 3, Making Sound – The Larynx, Voice Qualities.*** In this section, we will show you how to access these different voice qualities through the use of emotion.

The voice qualities are:

speech
cry/tilt
sob/tilt
falsetto
belt

The following diagrams show the relative positions of the thyroid, cricoid and arytenoid cartilages and their effect upon the vocal folds in order to create the voice qualities. The relationship of the parts of the larynx to each

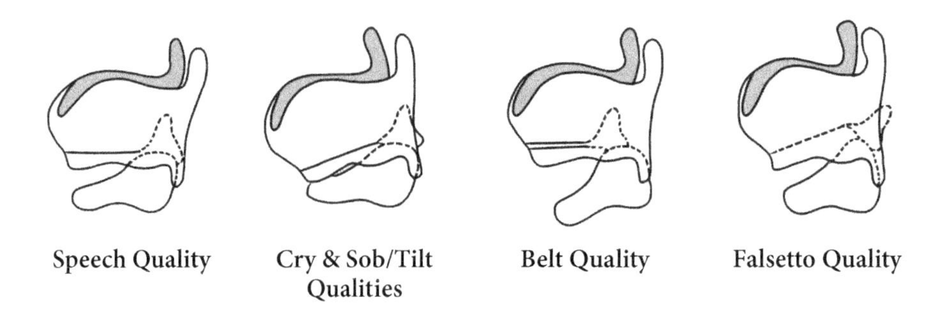

[Diagram: Laryngeal Postures for Voice Qualities]

Fig. 15 Laryngeal Postures for Voice Qualities; Image reference can be found on P. 223

other when making voice qualities is called laryngeal posture.

The most easily recognised quality is ***sob/tilt.*** The larynx is lowered and the thyroid is tilted, which positions the vocal folds at an angle above the airflow. As a result the voice sounds mellow and darker in timbre. It is one of the most important qualities needed for classical singing. The emotion which helps the student to achieve this quality is to think "sad".

Sob/tilt and cry/tilt qualities are similar. The thyroid cartilage is tilted, but for ***cry/tilt,*** the larynx is relatively higher in the throat. The emotion which helps the student to achieve this quality is to think "happy".

Pure ***speech quality*** is in what may be called the "neutral" position. The larynx is neither high nor low in the throat, and there is no tilting of any of the cartilages. The true vocal folds sit in a horizontal position above the airflow. They are closely adducted and generally thicker than for sob/tilt or cry/tilt, so the voice sounds clear and direct. There is no particular emotion attached to this quality, but the energy is higher and it works best in the middle range of the voice.

Falsetto is the easiest quality of them all. It requires little effort to produce and functions best in the upper range of the voice. The sound produced is breathy because the vocal folds are not fully together. The arytenoid cartilages have flipped backwards, which raises the back end of the vocal folds making them stretched and stiffened. Men's voices sound feminine in this quality. There is no particular emotion associated with this quality, but it is very effective for producing soft high notes.

Belt quality may be described as taking speech quality to a higher level of energy and pitch. The larynx is higher in the throat; the thyroid cartilage does not tilt, so the vocal folds are in a horizontal position above the airflow. The cricoid cartilage tilts, which makes the vocal folds thicker. The sound is therefore louder and exciting. It is very close to a yell, but must be more controlled. Emotions run high in belt quality and it can only be used at the upper end of the range. The high pitches in belt quality are achieved by increased air pressure, as the true vocal folds are short and thick. Because of the energy level and need for control, it is not recommended for young singers.

Twang

The twang sound is produced by the action of the aryepiglottic sphincter muscle, and is sometimes referred to as another voice quality. This is not actually the case. Twang alters the resonating chamber of the laryngo-pharynx and can affect the sound in all of the voice qualities, making the voice sound brighter and clearly projected. It is a resonating device. ***(See The Essential Anatomy, Chapter 4, Modifying Sound – The Resonators, Twang and the Aryepiglottic Sphincter)***

Twang is present in many languages and accents, and is a safe way of using the voice. It can be clearly heard in the American and Australian accents, and in the Chinese languages. Twang acts as a natural amplifying system for the voice, with the added benefit of requiring less work from the true vocal folds. Twang can be used in all voice qualities and is a resonating device which makes the sound brighter and more intense.

Learning to use twang gives the singer a great advantage, as less energy is used in producing sound with this resonator. Through twang, the singer can access the higher notes of the range more easily and safely, as the true vocal folds are in a thin state. The singer can slide through transitions of register from low to middle and middle to high with greater ease.

Volume is achieved through resonance rather than just the effort of increased air pressure. Twang has the added benefit of clear projection, whatever the volume.

Vibrato

Vibrato is a slight variation of pitch around a central note, arising from the free vibration of the true vocal folds and the larynx itself. As has been mentioned in this section, the rise and fall of the larynx affects pitch. For vibrato, the larynx is gently moving on the airflow, and those slight movements cause the variation of pitch around the central note. The larynx has to be supported, but not gripped. The voice consequently sounds warmer and rounder.

If the movement of the larynx were to increase due to loss of support or too much air pressure, the variation of pitch around the central note would widen, creating a wobble. Sometimes this is referred to as a "friendly voice" – one which waves at the audience! ***(See Troubleshooting, Chapter 2, Recognising and Remedying Vocal Difficulties, Wobble)***

Absence of vibrato creates the "white" voiced straight tone which is currently popular among exponents of Early Music. ***(See Appendix, Song Genres and***

Styles) Relating the sound to the anatomy, this can be described as thin-fold speech quality, with a predominance of head sinus resonance.
Vibrato naturally occurs with thyroid tilt, when singing with sob/tilt or cry/tilt quality. Speech quality does not lend itself to vibrato, but it may be added deliberately to the tone for effect, particularly at the end of phrases. In this case, care must be taken that vibrato does not become extreme and turn into a wobble.

When the airflow is not properly controlled by the breath support system, the larynx may grip, and so produce a "bleat", a fast, unpleasant vibrato. ***(See Troubleshooting, Chapter 2, Recognising and Remedying Vocal Difficulties, Bleat)*** The voice is seriously affected when the vocal folds try to control the airflow at the same time as they are vibrating to speak or sing. Control of airflow in singing should be done by the breath support system, not by the larynx.

Trill

Trill is a controlled vibrato produced by a well-supported, free larynx. It rises and falls rapidly in the throat to encompass two notes either a semi-tone or a full tone apart. The trill is viewed in the bel canto school as the finished product of a well-trained and well-produced voice.

Relating Speech to Singing

Chapter Two

Speech quality is the core of the singing voice! Just as a dancer is trained from first position, the singer must develop all other voice qualities in relation to speech quality. It is essential that healthy speech quality be established in the singer from the start, in order to access the widest range of voice qualities in his or her singing.

The singing voice uses the same mechanisms as the speaking voice, but in a slightly different way. If you can speak, it is probable that you can sing. Relating the singing voice to the speaking voice in training can be helpful in getting a beginner started. The next paragraphs contain very basic information, and will be useful to the teacher who has a student with little or no prior experience of singing.

In speech quality, the thyroid and cricoid cartilages are not tilted (neutral position). The vocal folds are in a horizontal position above the airflow. This quality works well in the middle range of the voice; it requires a greater level of energy at higher pitches.

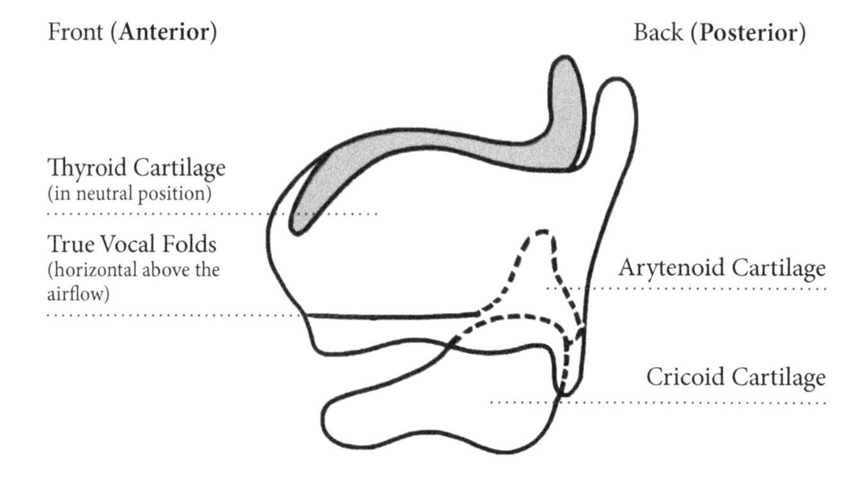

[Diagram: Thyroid Cartilage in Neutral Position (Speech Quality)]

Thyroid cartilage in neutral position (speech quality)

Fig. 16 Thyroid Cartilage in Neutral Position; Image reference can be found on P. 223

Singing is Speaking with a Tune

Tunes require a wider range of pitch than ordinary conversation. As has been mentioned previously, pitch is governed by two main factors:
the position of the larynx in the throat (high or low),
the air pressure in the thorax created by the breath support system

Exercise:
Say: "Mary had a little lamb" in a normal tone of voice

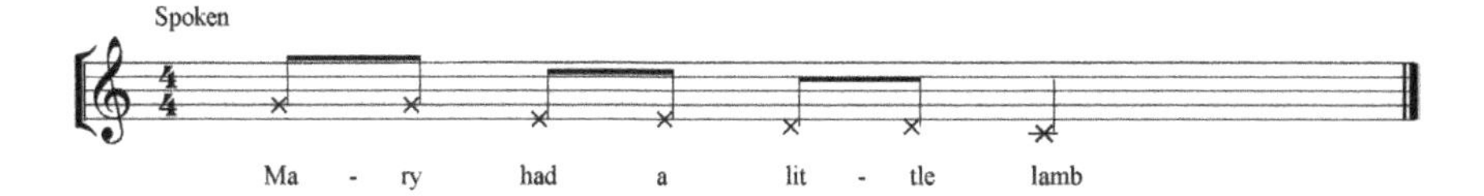

Exercise:
Repeat this robotically, on a monotone.

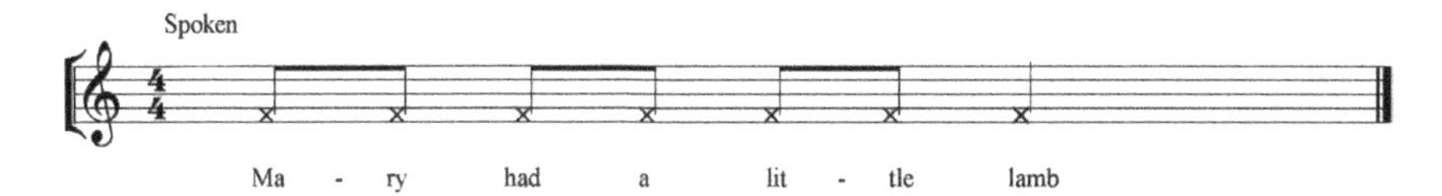

On comparing the two, it will be noted that there is the hint of a tune in ordinary speech, which is called "inflection".

Exercise:
Repeat the phrase, this time exaggerating the pitch of the speech.

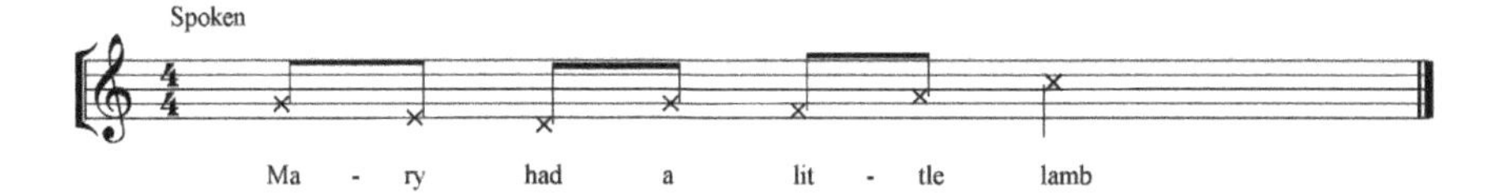

The tune becomes more explicit.

Exercise:
Place a finger on the larynx and repeat the exaggerated speech. (You may observe the movement of the larynx in a mirror if you prefer)

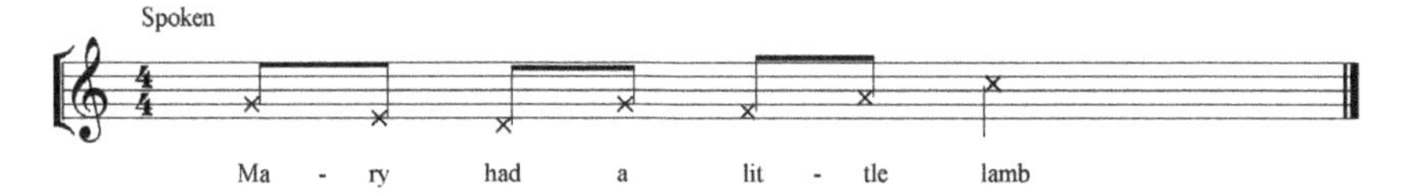

You will feel that the larynx rises in the throat as the pitch rises, and the larynx lowers in the throat as the pitch lowers. It is important to be aware of this movement, as it plays such a major role in pitching and voice quality.

Phrases are generally longer in singing than in speech.

Singing requires longer outflow of breath and therefore more muscular activity from the breathing and support systems of the body. This can be explored in the following way.

Exercise:
Say : "Mary had a little lamb" in a normal tone of voice.

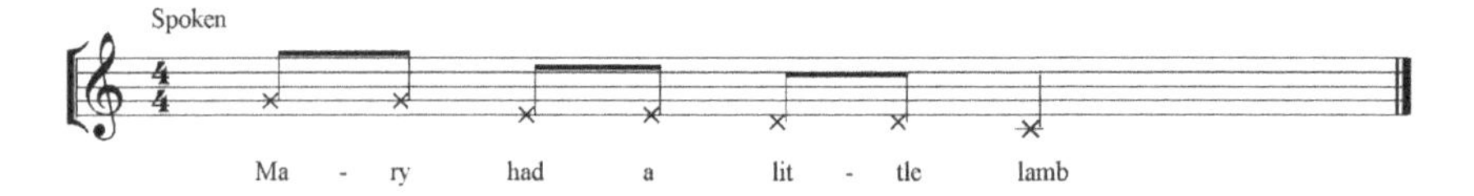

Exercise:
Repeat this phrase VERY SLOWLY, taking as long as you can.

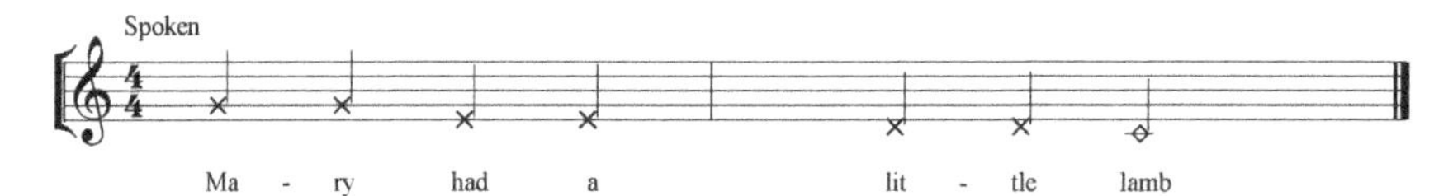

You will notice that you are using a lot more breath to say the phrase slowly. In order to sustain the longer phrase, you have to manage the airflow in a more controlled way. This is now closer to the breath support required for singing than for ordinary speaking.

Exercise:
Repeat the phrase very slowly, exaggerating the pitch changes.

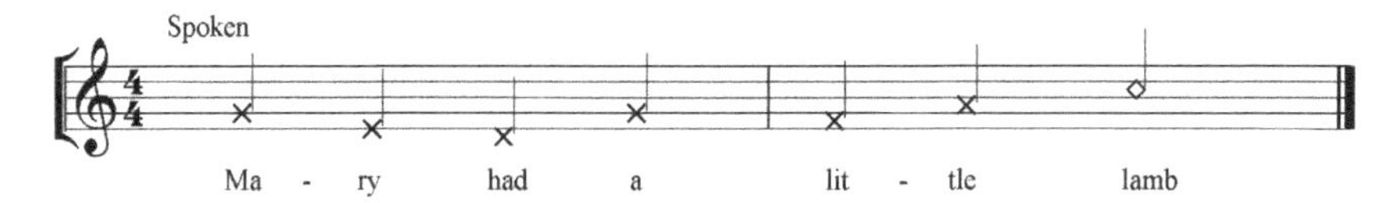

When the longer phrase is combined with the exaggerated pitch changes, you are close to singing. Perfecting the control over breath and pitch is a basic goal of training the singing voice.

Singing carries an emotional content which is more exaggerated than in speech.

Singing is much more emotional than speaking. A poem is enhanced when a melody is added; just think of the work of Schubert, Fauré, Quilter … the list is endless. The emotional content of singing is conveyed by changes within the larynx. These physical movements are explained in the chapter on ***Voice Qualities*** earlier in this section.

Cry/tilt and Sob/tilt are two voice qualities used extensively in classical singing ***(See Appendix, Song Genres and Styles)***, and are of particular value in helping to extend the range of the voice. Your voice will sound different in each of the following exercises, even though the phrase remains the same. This is because an emotional content has been brought into play.

A sad tone of voice is created by tilting the thyroid cartilage and lowering the larynx in the throat. This makes a sound like sobbing.

A happy tone of voice is created by tilting the thyroid cartilage and raising the larynx in the throat. It is useful to think of this sound as a happy cry.

Exercise:
Say: "Mary had a little lamb" in a normal tone of voice.

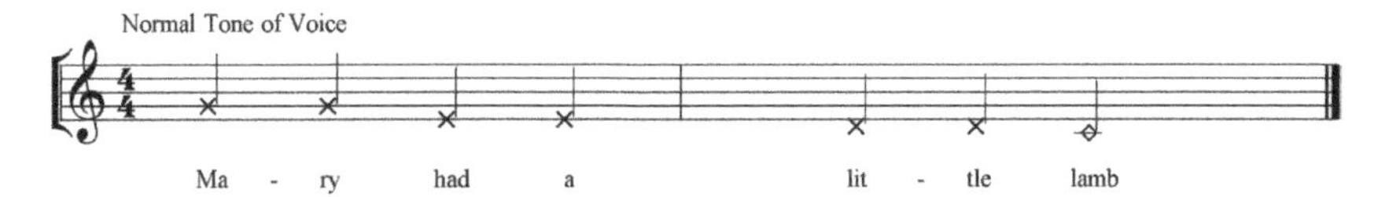

Exercise:
Say: "Mary had a little lamb" in a sad tone of voice.

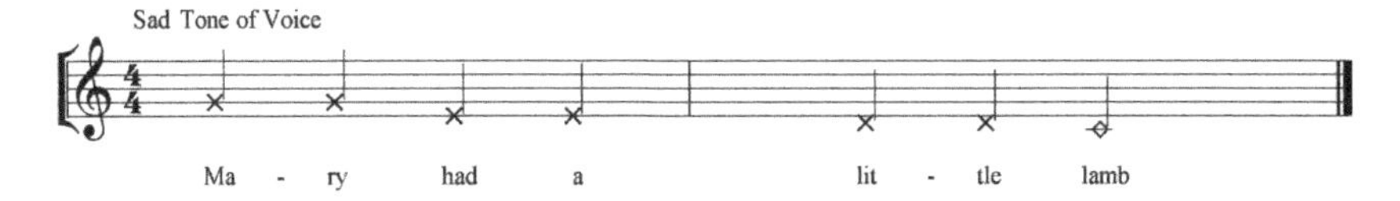

Exercise:
Say: "Mary had a little lamb" in a happy tone of voice.

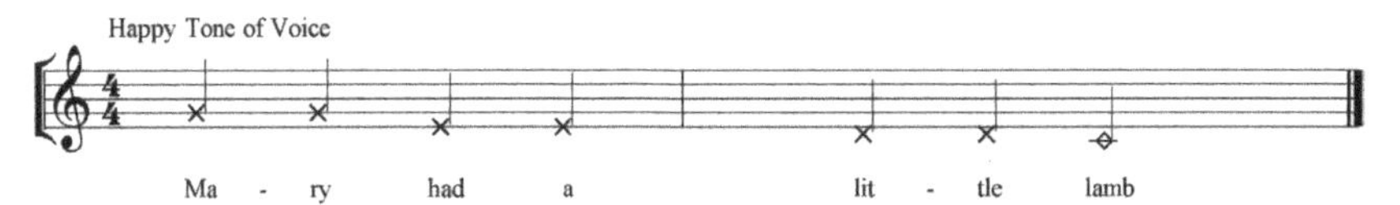

When you repeat the above exercises with extended pitch and length of phrase, the differences in voice qualities become even more striking. The different voice qualities are used more intensively in singing than in ordinary speech, and change as the emotional content of the song unfolds.

Voice qualities require more energy to sustain in singing than is needed in speaking. The question of stamina now arises. You need to be able to understand how the vocal mechanisms are being used to create these sounds, in order to train a singer to use them consistently well and safely. ***(See The Fast Track, Chapter 3, The Basic of Teaching Singing, Stamina Building; and also Chapter 5, Practice, later in this section)***

Turning Speech into Singing

Chapter Three

Voice Qualities in a Tune

It is now time to use the voice qualities in a tune. "Happy Birthday to You" is an all-time favourite:

Exercise:
Sing: "Happy Birthday To You" in speech quality (normal tone of voice with no emotion).

Laryngeal posture:
the thyroid and cricoid cartilages are in neutral position
the vocal folds are horizontal to the airflow

Exercise:
Sing: "Happy Birthday To You" in sob/tilt quality (a sad tone of voice with a low larynx).

Laryngeal posture:
the thyroid cartilage is tilted forwards in relation to the cricoid
the larynx is lower in the throat than for speech

Exercise:
Sing: "Happy Birthday To You" in cry/tilt quality (a very happy tone of voice with a higher larynx).

Laryngeal posture:
the thyroid cartilage is tilted forwards in relation to the cricoid cartilage
the larynx is higher in the throat than for speech

Although the above are only exercises to practise the use of three voice qualities, it is clear that the song has been subtly changed each time by adding an emotion. When we put words and music together and add an emotion, the breath support system must work harder in order to sustain the singing.

What Is Good Singing?

Chapter Four

Generally we can all recognise good singing by the following criteria:

the singing is in tune
the voice sounds free
the voice sounds clear
there is a wide range of pitch without strain
the words are distinct
the meaning and emotion of the song are communicated

The Singing is in Tune

As has been previously explained in this section and in the section ***The Essential Anatomy***, singing in tune is dependent on

1. **the position of the larynx in the throat (high or low)**
2. **combined with the pressure of air in the lungs**
3. **which is controlled by the muscles of the breath support system.**

These three all work together in balance.

The position of the larynx in the throat combines with air pressure in order to pitch a note. As pitch rises in any voice quality, the larynx rises in the throat and the air pressure increases. Increases and decreases in the air pressure also affect the volume (loudness and softness) of a note. It is important when training the voice not to allow volume to increase as the pitch rises, because the higher notes will then become difficult to produce. The larynx may not be able to move properly in the throat if the air pressure is too great. The nature of this sound is often referred to as being "driven", or "over-blown".

The relationship between the position of the larynx and air pressure is variable. For example, it is possible to sing high notes with a relatively low larynx, as with sob/tilt. However, the air pressure required would be greater than for the same note in cry/tilt which uses a higher larynx. It is easier to sing higher notes in cry/tilt, because the air pressure required would be less. Loud high notes with a low larynx may be exciting, but they require a great deal of physical strength, and are tiring for both the larynx and the breath support system.

These are the notes which most often tend to be out of tune.
In order to establish the principles of good tuning for notes in the middle range of the voice, it is important to work with the larynx in the speech quality position (mid-throat, neither high nor low). All other voice qualities can be accessed from speech quality, and good singing is a blend of those qualities with speech.

The following exercises are useful for helping beginners who have trouble pitching notes. Some people who do have trouble pitching say they are tone deaf. Real tone deafness is a rare condition. Most of these people need to be shown how to find notes. Singing in tune can be taught. ***(See ALSO Practical Singing for All Musicians, Chapter 2, Aural Training – Using Your Ears to Find Your Voice, Recognising Pitch)***

Exercise:
Slide the voice through the middle range on the following vowels.
The starting note can be played on an instrument, or vocalised by the teacher.

ah as in father
eh as in head
ee as in seat
o as in hot
oo as in would

There could be a visual cue from the teacher to indicate the pitch at which the student is singing. For example, the teacher may raise and lower an index finger as the student slides through the range of notes.

This exercise can now be refined by using fixed pitches as notated below.

Exercise:
The teacher should play or sing a note. The student slides upwards or downwards until they arrive at the note played or sung.

This exercise should also be accompanied by the physical activity of the moving finger. The teacher's finger indicates the pitch of the note which they have played; the student's finger shows the movement towards the note until it is finally reached.

The greater the distance the finger moves, the wider the intervals. The higher the finger, the higher the pitch, and so on.

Visual cues are very useful for correcting poor tuning. If the singer is under the note, the rising finger indicates that the pitch has to rise; the descending finger indicates that the pitch must fall. Practising the above exercises helps to train the ear and enables the singer to gain fine control over tuning.

The Voice Sounds Free

The vibration of air caused by the action of the true vocal folds produces a sound wave. If nothing interferes with the sound wave, we hear it as a free sound. If the sound wave is interfered with, that freedom is lost. The voice sounds strained and unpleasant.

The first level of interference with the free sound can be at the level of the true vocal folds. As has been explained in ***The Essential Anatomy***, situated above these are the false vocal folds. Their natural tendency is to bear downwards, interfering with the action of the true vocal folds, which distorts the sound wave. This is called constriction. ***(See The Essential Anatomy Chapter 3, Making Sound – The Larynx The True Vocal Folds; The False Vocal Folds)***

Constriction can occur when a singer is nervous, or when greater energy is required, as in singing loudly or singing high notes. The opposite to constriction is ***retraction***. This is where the false vocal folds are pulled out of the way of the true vocal folds. The singer must be trained to retract the false vocal folds at all times, so that any interference does not occur. The action of the false vocal folds not only restricts the freedom of the sound, but it may damage the true vocal folds themselves.

The false vocal folds naturally retract during sobbing and laughing. Laughing is more fun, so use this to practise retraction; the feeling in the throat is one of width. The following exercises train the singer to gain control over the action of the false vocal folds to produce retraction.

Exercise 1:
Laugh silently and with energy for 10 seconds.

Focus on the muscular work involved without the distraction of sound. Be aware of the muscular activity involved in the throat in order to keep the false vocal folds out of the way!

Learning by the feel of this activity rather than by the sound produced will help you gain better control over retraction.

Exercise 2:
Now voice the laugh, and then turn the laugh into a sung tone on a vowel of choice.

Begin this with one repeated note, then use a sequence of notes as shown below. It is important to keep the emotion of the laugh throughout, as this reinforces the retraction.

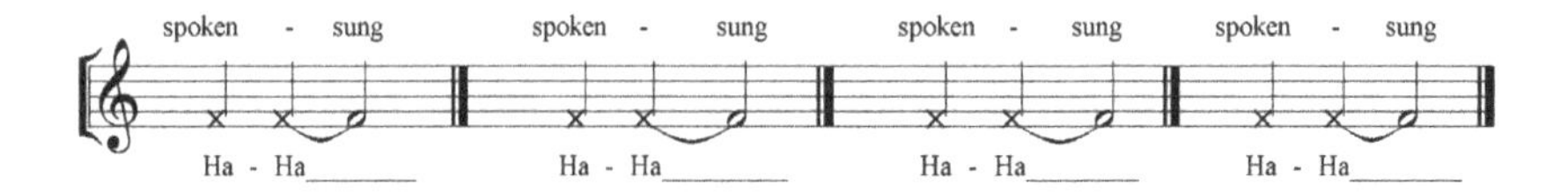

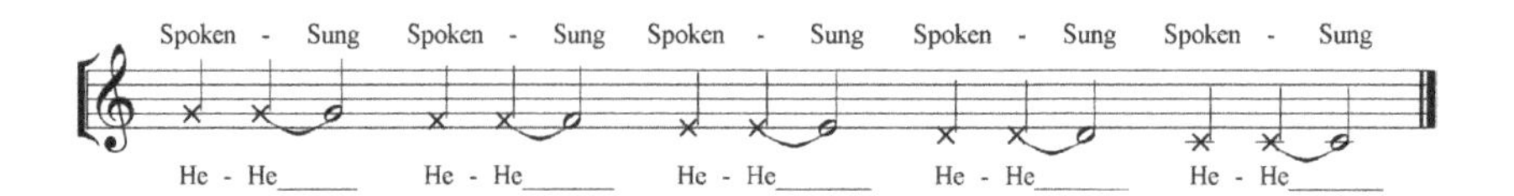

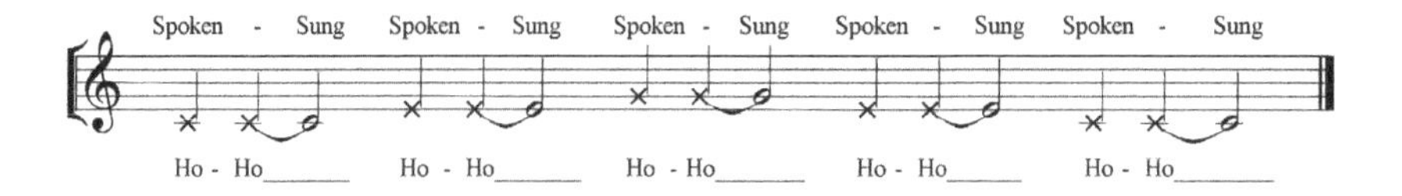

The true vocal folds themselves can act to interfere with the sound wave. It must be remembered that the larynx is a valve constrictor, the primary function of which is to block airflow! The true vocal folds close tightly to prevent food or drink entering the airway. Every time we swallow, they close.

If the true vocal folds try to control air while they are vibrating, the voice sounds squeezed and definitely not free. It may sound like a bleat, a fast, unpleasant vibrato arising from this incorrect control of airflow. ***(See Troubleshooting, Chapter 2, Recognising and Remedying Vocal Difficulties, Bleat)***

In order for the sound to remain free, it is essential that the outward airflow is controlled by the muscles of the breath support system, as described in The Essential Anatomy section. ***(See The Essential Anatomy Chapter 2, Breathing – Breath Support)***

Creating an obstruction to airflow with an unvoiced consonant sound, such as FFF and SHH, encourages the breath support muscles to work vigorously. With an unvoiced consonant, the vocal folds are not vibrating.

Repeating this activity with a voiced consonant, such as VVV and ZZZ, links the breath support to a sound, without placing undue pressure on the vocal folds.

These exercises help to develop a healthy balance between vocal fold activity, airflow and bodily support

Unvoiced Singing Exercise.

Exercise:
Think of the pitches on the stave below, and then make a strong "FFF". Make sure that the true vocal folds do not vibrate. The only sound that you should here is the escape of air from the lips. The notes may be played on the piano during this exercise.

Voiced Singing Exercises.

Exercise 1:
Get the muscles working by creating a blockage to the outward airflow, using the upper teeth on the lower lip. Make sure that the true vocal folds do vibrate ("VVV").

Feel the muscles at the sides of the abdomen between the rib cage and the hip bones. Notice that they adjust to accommodate the differences in pitch.

The point of the exercise is to compress the air. Indeed, the sound should be contained and buzzing, like a bee in a bottle.

Exercise 2:
Make the "VVV". Slide the pitches as indicated on the stave below. Feel the muscles at the sides of the abdomen between the rib cage and the hip bones. Notice that they adjust to accommodate the differences in pitch.

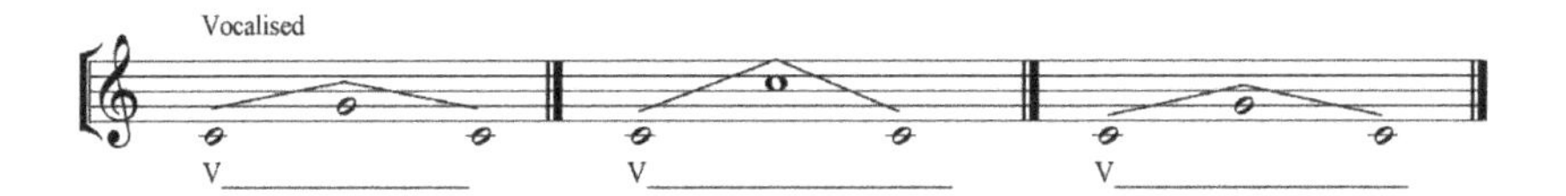

Exercise 3:
Repeat using "ZZZ"
Feel the muscles at the sides of the abdomen between the rib cage and the hip bones. Notice that they adjust to accommodate the differences in pitch.

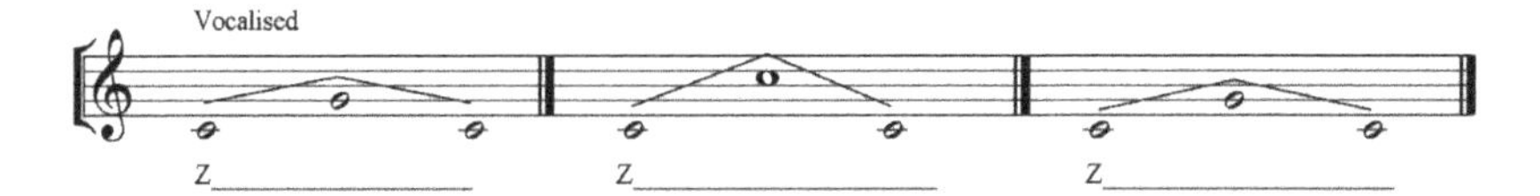

Exercise 4:
Make the "VVV". Vocalise the pitches as indicated on the stave and notice the work in the body as well as the movement of the larynx.

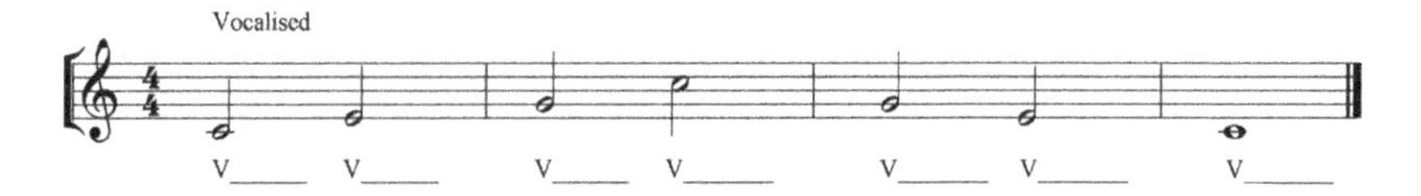

Exercise 5:
Repeat using "ZZZ". Notice the work in the body as well as the movement of the larynx.

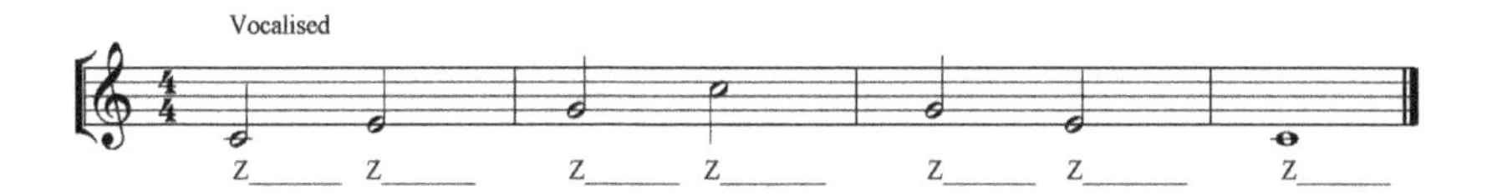

Exercise 6:
This time, open the voice from the "VVV" to a vowel as indicated below. The muscles of the breath support system will be activated by the "VVV" and must remain energised for the open vowel.

Exercise 7:
Repeat using "ZZZ". The muscles of the breath support system will be activated by the "ZZZ" and must remain energised for the open vowel.

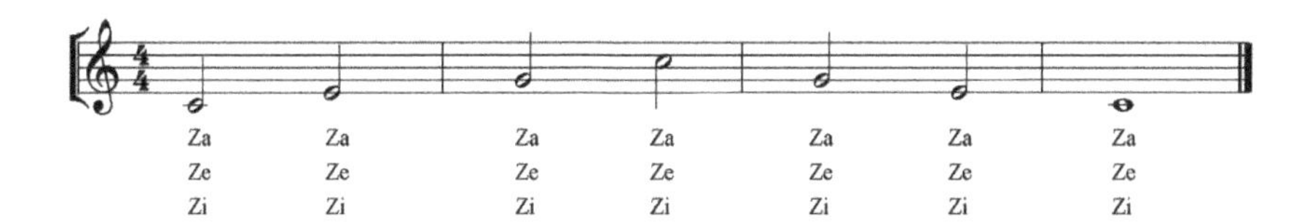

The second level of possible interference with the pure sound wave may occur above the true vocal folds, in the resonators. This is dealt with in the next chapter.

The Voice Sounds Clear

A clear voice is the result of a pure sound wave, free of interference, enhanced by the use of the resonators. If the voice sounds muffled and unclear, it is usually because the resonators are not being properly controlled.

An obvious example of this is nasality, which makes the voice sound weak and dull, and restricts the range of emotional colour. Lack of muscle tone in the walls of the pharynx also produces a weak and muffled sound. ***(See The Essential Anatomy, Chapter 4, Modifying Sound – The Resonators)***

Naturally clear sound can further be affected by tension in the root of the tongue, as well as the tongue's position in the throat and mouth. For example, if the tongue is too far back in the throat, as with a yawn, it will block the pharynx and impede its resonance.

And finally, of course, the voice will be muffled and unclear if the airflow is not properly supported.

Nasality

A clear sound naturally emerges through the mouth. However, certain consonants in English such as "ng", "m", "n", make the sound emerge through the nose. Some languages, such as French, have vowels which are nasal. The mechanism which controls this nasality is the ***soft palate***.

When the soft palate is lowered, the sound emerges through the nose. The sound "ng" cuts off the mouth resonance almost entirely. You can observe this by pinching and releasing your nose as you make the "ng" sound. The sound will be blocked when the nose is pinched. You can also put your hand over your mouth as you make the sound. Because the sound is coming through the nose, not the mouth, the sound is not affected very much at all.

When the soft palate is raised, the sound emerges through the mouth. So, to avoid unnecessary nasality, the soft palate must be trained to lift out of the way when it is not needed.

Soft Palate Exercise

Exercise:
Make the sound "ng-gah". The "g" of "gah" should be well energised.

The sound "ng" is made predominately through the nose, as the soft palate is down. The "gah" sound should issue through the mouth; it is the upward movement of the soft palate which allows this to happen.

The movement of the soft palate is controlled by two sets of muscles within the soft palate itself. If, for example, the regional accent is nasal, these muscles may not be developed enough to work efficiently. The singer must learn to gain control of the soft palate on order to ensure clarity of tone.

The Neck and Pharynx

The clarity of tone may also be impaired by a tendency of the walls of the pharynx to collapse. This is caused by a lack of proper energy in the muscles of the neck, referred to as the scaffolding muscles in ***The Essential Anatomy*** section. These may be chronically underpowered because of poor habitual speech patterns, or even regional accent.

The larynx needs to be properly anchored by these scaffolding muscles in order to function efficiently and produce clear sound. When the walls of the pharynx are energised by the engagement of these muscles, the sound wave arising from the true vocal folds is enhanced by this resonator. The voice then sounds clear. If the walls of the pharynx are weak, the voice will sound dull and muffled. ***(See The Essential Anatomy, Chapter 3, Making Sound – The Larynx, Component Parts of the Larynx)***

Exercise:
Place your hand around the base of your neck, and lightly apply pressure to your forehead with the other hand.

You will observe that the muscles in the neck contract and anchor downwards, connecting more firmly to the clavicles and sternum. The walls of the pharynx are now energised.

The Tongue

The tongue is not just one muscle, but a combination of several which work together to comprise the fastest moving organ in the body. It is a very flexible organ, and allows the singer to alter the shape of the mouth and pharynx with speed and precision.

The tongue is capable of depressing the entire larynx by moving backwards and downwards, as in the act of swallowing. This is not helpful when you need to raise the larynx in order to sing a high note. The backward movement of the tongue can interfere with the free rise and fall of the larynx in the throat, and will muffle the sound.

Poor control of the tongue can cause lack of clarity in forming vowels. For example, an 'ee' vowel is formed when the back of the tongue is in a higher position, and an 'ah' vowel when the back of the tongue is in a lower position. If the tongue is backward and downward for both of these vowels, they cannot be clear. ***(See Troubleshooting, Chapter 2, Recognising and remedying Vocal Difficulties, Tension in the Root of the Tongue; Wrong Positioning of the Tongue)***

Exercise:
Place the tip of the tongue on the back of the lower front teeth. Then raise the back of the tongue so that the sides touch the upper molars at the back of the mouth.

Then say the "ee" vowel followed by the "ah" vowel. Notice the movement of the tongue as it changes position for each vowel.

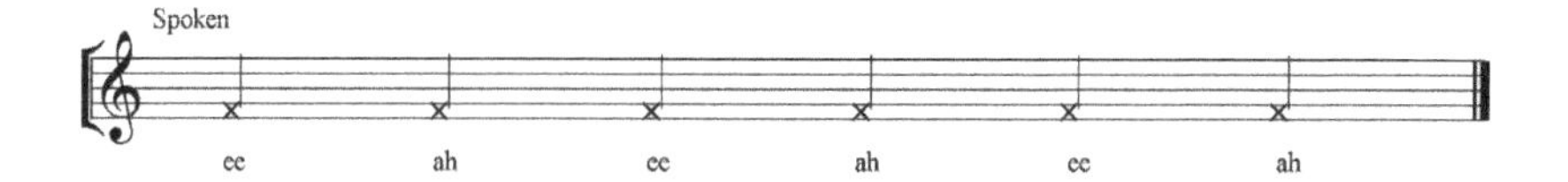

Tension in the Jaw and Tongue

Tension in the jaw often indicates that there is a corresponding tension at the root of the tongue. Tongue-root tension can make the voice sound gripped and unclear. The Italian school of bel canto insisted that singers worked intensively on the creation of pure vowel sounds. Vowels cannot be pure if there is tongue-root tension, as all vowels are formed by the action of the tongue along with the shape of the throat and mouth. Eradicating tongue-root tension will free the sound and allow the voice to be clear. ***(See Troubleshooting, Chapter 2, Recognising and remedying Vocal Difficulties, Tension in the Jaw; Tension in the Root of the Tongue)***

Exercise 1:

Say the "ee" vowel followed by the other vowels, this time sliding from one vowel to the other, taking care not to grip the jaw. The tongue is capable of moving independently from the jaw.

This exercise will reveal those singers who have some tongue or jaw tension, because they will find it difficult to move the tongue independently of the jaw. They should persist with the exercises very gently to overcome the problem.

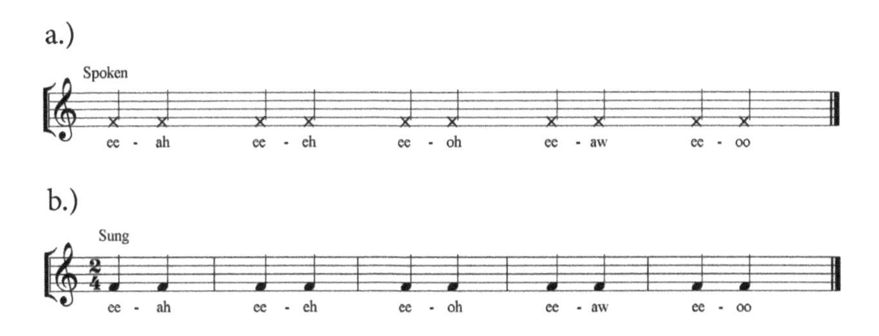

Exercise 2:

To encourage release of clenched muscles in the jaw, rest the upper teeth on the lower lip as if to make an "F" and suck to create a vacuum. Then open the mouth against the resistance caused by the vacuum. There will be a popping sound. The muscles which normally clench the jaw will be released by this action.

Tension at the root of the tongue may also be addressed through use of the "L" consonant.

Exercise 3:
Place the tongue on the ridge behind the upper teeth (the alveolar ridge), as if to make the "L" sound.

Make an "H" sound followed by a voiced "L". The vocalised sound will be "H-L".

If this sounds gripped, it is because there is tension at the root of the tongue accompanied by insufficient airflow. The air must flow through the "H" sound and continue to flow as the "L" is pronounced. You will feel the scaffolding muscles in the neck anchoring onto the sternum and clavicles.

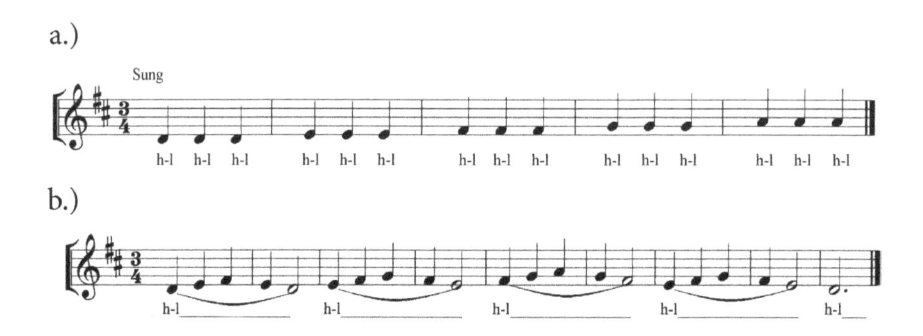

Practice these exercises gently to encourage the release of any muscles which are involuntarily contracting in the tongue and jaw.

There is a Wide Range of Pitch Without Strain

The singer can access the full vocal range if the larynx is able to move up and down in the throat freely. This can be encouraged by ***sirening***, which must be done very softly, so that the larynx moves with little air pressure.

Sirening

Sirening is a safe diagnostic tool as well as an effective exercise for the singing voice. It uses the fine edges of the true vocal folds with little air pressure and little muscular activity.

Sirening:

demonstrates the natural rise and fall of the larynx over the range

indicates the condition of the vocal folds and should be used on a daily basis
equalises the tension of the vocal folds
is a good gentle warm-up exercise

Exercise:
Say the word "sing" making sure the "ng" is prolonged. The "i" vowel of "sing" raises the larynx in preparation for accessing the higher notes.

Select a note in the middle voice comfort zone and gently slide upwards and downwards, maintaining the "ng" throughout the range. The siren should never be loud.

Notice where the tongue is positioned when forming the "ng": the tip of the tongue is placed behind the lower front teeth, whilst the back of the tongue is raised. This allows maximum freedom for the larynx to rise and fall without any interference from the tongue. It is important to realise that an "ng" will always be nasal in tone.

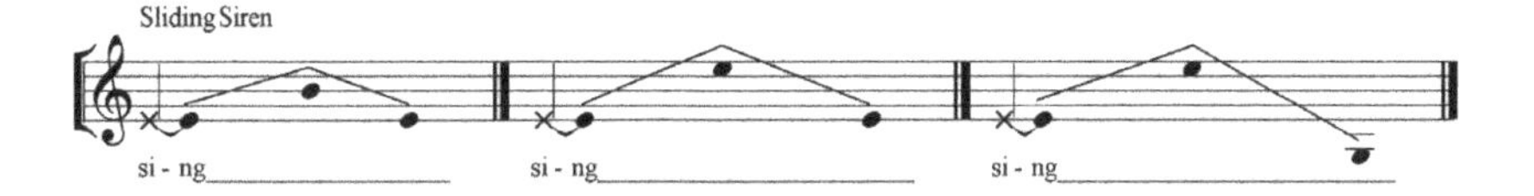

Relating Air Pressure to Pitch

Strain is a symptom of misplaced energy. There must be appropriate energy from the breathing and support mechanisms in order to access the full range. If there is not sufficient air pressure to attain the pitch, the notes will not be reached.

As louder sounds also require more air pressure, the following exercises should be practised at a moderate level of volume, so that the student learns to distinguish between the air pressure needed for pitch and that needed for volume. If the air pressure is too low, the voice will slip into falsetto, which is the easiest voice quality for high pitches, but not necessarily satisfying to the listener. ***(See The Fast Track, Chapter 3, The Basics of Teaching Singing, Breathing; The Essential Anatomy, Chapter 2, Breathing – Breath Support)***

The preparation for the following exercise is similar to that used earlier in this section.

Exercise:
Make the "VVV" sound (upper teeth on lower lip) in order to block the airflow primarily at the lip. This takes pressure away from the true vocal folds, as they do not fully close. It is important that the airflow is maintained on the "VVV" sound throughout the octave rise.

Pitch the lower note and slide the voice through to the upper note, maintaining the "VVV" sound.

The "VVV" ensures that the muscles used for anchoring the voice are properly engaged. To observe their activity, you should place your hands on your sides and hold firmly as you do the octave slides.

The breath support muscles will contract as the pitch rises. If there is little activity in these muscles, the voice will go into falsetto. Engaging the muscles more fully as the voice goes into the upper range ensures that strain will be taken away from the larynx. The breath must continue to flow.

Tilting the Thyroid Cartilage

Long vocal folds create higher frequencies than short vocal folds. In cry/tilt and sob/tilt voice qualities, the thyroid cartilage tilts forward in relation to the cricoid cartilage. This has the effect of lengthening the vocal folds, allowing them to create higher frequencies, making the higher notes easier to attain. ***(See: The Essential Anatomy, Chapter 3, Making Sound – The Larynx, Voice Qualities)***

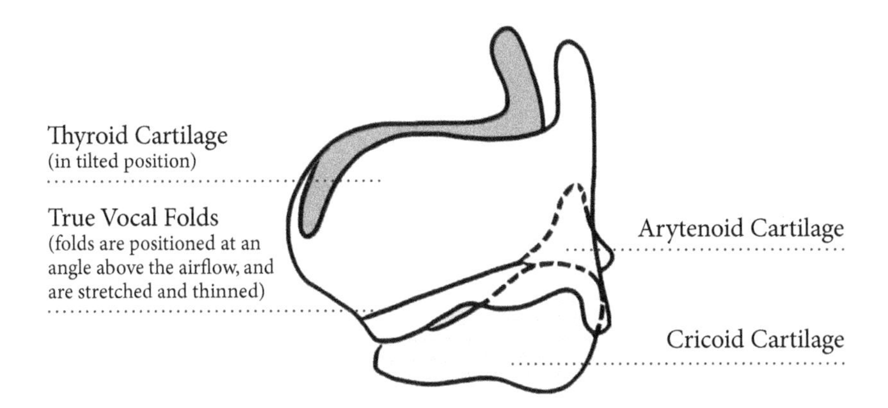

[Diagram: Thyroid Cartilage in Tilted Position (Cry/Tilt And Sob/Tilt Qualities)] hyroid cartilage in tilted position (cry/tilt and sob/tilt qualities)

Fig. 17 Thyroid Cartilage in Titled Position; Image reference can be found on P. 223

Because the vocal folds are also thinner in this position, they require less air pressure relative to pitch, and allow the larynx more freedom of movement.

Cry/Tilt Exercises

In the following exercises, the thyroid cartilage is tilted forward and the larynx is relatively high in the throat. This helps to attain higher notes comfortably and with little air pressure.

With these exercises, the abdominal and back muscles should be engaged, as they are in the "VVV" exercises. The higher the pitch, the greater the muscular work.

Exercise:
A cry is not necessarily sad or unhappy. There can also be a cry of joy. In order to raise the larynx, it helps to think of a happy cry.

The "miaouw" is useful because it takes you through a series of different vowel positions in a single word.

For girls and boys with unbroken voices, take the exercise sequence initially to the upper F.

For boys with newly broken voices, go to the D.

For adult singers, explore the comfortable range of the voice as it exists, and work to extend this without forcing the voice.

Keep working on this exercise so that the range extends.

a.)

b.)

Sob/Tilt Exercises

In the following exercises, the thyroid cartilage is tilted forward and the larynx is relatively low in the throat. The lower larynx means that the breath support system has to be engaged to a greater degree. Extend the range upward, whilst remaining comfortable.

With these exercises, the abdominal and back muscles should be engaged, as they are in the "VVV" exercises. The higher the pitch, the greater the muscular work.

Exercise:
For the sob, it helps to think of a sad emotion. This will naturally lower the larynx in the throat, and tilt the thyroid cartilage forward. Note that there is more work required from the breath support system than for the cry/tilt exercises.

For girls and boys with unbroken voices, take the exercise sequence initially to the upper F.

For boys with newly broken voices, go to the D.

For adult singers, explore the comfortable range of the voice as it exists, and work to extend this without forcing the voice.

The Words are Distinct

In good singing, words should be distinct, so that the listener can understand what the singer is communicating. The emotional content of a song is carried by the vowels through the voice qualities. The sense of the words is carried by the consonants, which also reinforce the emotional content. The singer may be producing beautiful vowel sounds, but if the consonants are not properly energised, the meaning will not carry to the listener.

Clarity of diction requires heightened energy from all of the articulators, which are the tongue, teeth and lips. This heightened energy should not be allowed to become tension, which interferes with the production of the singing sound. Such tension may arise in the tongue and jaw, as we have seen earlier in this section. The singer must avoid over-articulation, which is a distortion and exaggeration of mouth shapes, leading to jaw tension. True clarity of diction comes from properly energised consonants, not from distorted vowels.

All consonants, whether voiced or unvoiced, may potentially be pitched! For example, it is easily demonstrated that "V", a voiced consonant, may be pitched; it is not so easily demonstrated, but equally true, that its unvoiced equivalent, "F", also may be pitched. Legato singing is not only singing the vowels in tune, but the consonants also, whether voiced or unvoiced. This is necessary so that the meaning is not lost and the communication is complete without destroying the legato line.

Exercise 1:

This exercise shows that there is an engagement of the breath support system for both voiced and unvoiced consonants, and that the level of energy rises as the pitch rises.

Make the "VVV" sound on the ascending slides, followed by the "FFF" sounds, where the rising pitch has to be imagined.

Although the "FFF" sound is not voiced, the abdominal muscles will contract increasingly as the imagined pitch rises.

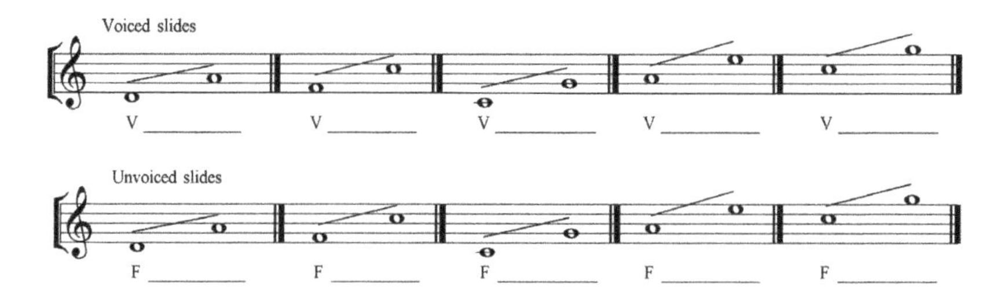

Exercise 2:
For this exercise, open the voice from the "VVV" to a vowel as indicated below. The muscles of the abdomen will be activated by the "VVV" and must remain so for the open vowel.
Repeat using "FFF". Although the "FFF" sound is not voiced, the abdominal muscles will contract increasingly as the pitch rises.

Voiced:

Unvoiced:

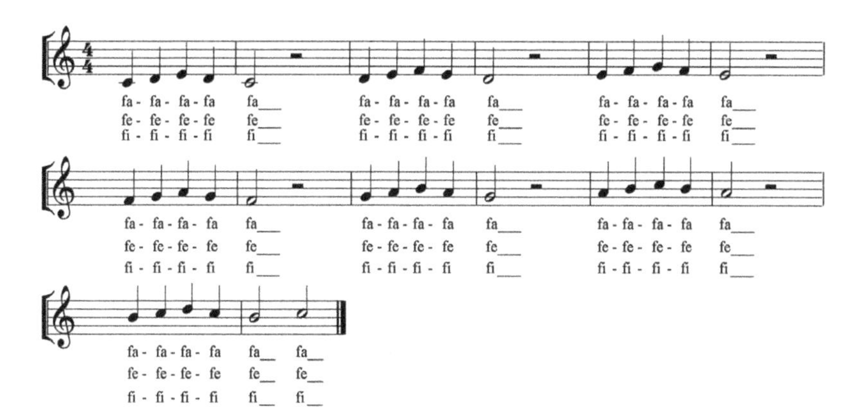

The above exercises may be adapted and used with other matched voiced and unvoiced consonants, and with other vowels. The energy, both in the mouth and in the body, must be maintained on the consonant, whether voiced or not!

Voiced Consonants	**Unvoiced Consonants**
B, D, G, J (DZ), V, Z	**P, T, K, SH, F, S**

The Meaning and Emotion of the Song are Communicated

The singer must have a personal response to the song if meaning and emotion are to be communicated. The teacher can help this process along by encouraging the singer to read and understand the text, independent of the music. Words and music are processed on different sides of the brain. Both should be explored separately before bringing them together in performance.

Emotions affect the larynx, the varying parts of which have been explained in ***The Essential Anatomy*** section. In order to communicate emotion through singing, the student must be able to control these moving parts voluntarily. Voice qualities arise naturally from an emotion – happiness, sadness, surprise, anger etc. Identifying the emotions contained within a song opens the way to interpretation through use of the voice qualities. Applying various emotional responses to the song enables the singer to exercise control of the different voice qualities. ***(See Making Music, Chapter 2, Putting It All Together, Choosing voice Qualities)***

Exercise:
Sing "Happy Birthday" with these emotions:
Happy – to your best friend (cry/tilt quality)
Sad – you don't want to be at this birthday party (sob/tilt quality)
Surprised – you were given the biggest birthday present (energised speech quality)
Highly excited – it was the birthday present you wanted most of all (very high energy speech quality)

The energy which the singer brings to the performance greatly influences the success of the communication with an audience. For example, if ordinary conversation requires a certain level of energy, singing to an audience will require much more! If that energy is not present, the communication will be weak.

It is very frustrating for the listener if a speaker stands before a group of thirty people and speaks with the energy he or she would use when speaking to ONE other person. The remaining twenty-nine feel excluded. If the act of speaking to an audience of thirty requires the energy level to be raised, the act of singing requires it to be raised even higher.

Singing is much more energetic than speaking. If the energy is not at the correct level, the performance will not be communicated. Please note that energy does not necessarily mean volume. It is more a matter of intensity.
(See Performance, Chapter 1)

Practice

Chapter Five

The Importance of Practice

Practice is an essential part of training the singing voice. It works in so many ways. The exercises presented in this section are designed to build the instrument. Other musicians are presented with their instrument all ready to play. They only have to learn how to do this.

The singer has to build a voice as well as learn how to use it. The repetition of exercises in practice sessions builds up muscle memory so that singing becomes easier and the singer can move on to more advanced levels. Stamina, the ability to sustain energy through the singing, develops only through practice.

How Long Should I Practise?

Singers frequently ask: "For how long should I practise, and how often?" The teacher should respond to this according to the stage of development and the age of the singer, as well as consideration of the task in hand. For example, a singer preparing for Grade 8 would need to spend a greater amount of time on learning the music than one taking Grade 5. All repertoire presents challenges of different degrees in technical, musical, characterisation and interpretative areas.

The type of practice undertaken should be divided into two main areas, technical and musical. Where a singer has to build a song into the voice, the advice would be "little and often", as the body needs to recover after each practice session. Stamina grows when energetic muscular activity is followed by a recovery period. Ten minutes of concentrated practice on a daily basis will produce better results than one long session per week. ***(See The Fast track, Chapter 3, The Basics of Teaching Singing, Stamina Building; Performance, Chapter 1)***

What Should I Practise?

The singer should take two or three exercises given in a previous lesson and work at those to build them into the voice. They may be repeated three or four times during the practise session. Then move on to a song. If you are learning a new song, take a small section and repeat the phrases. In the first stages of learning a song, resist looking at the entire song all in one practise session. Taking smaller sections of a song in any one practise session will speed up the process of committing the words and the music to memory. ***(See Performance, Chapter 2, Memorising)***

For songs which you already know, take a phrase which presents a technical challenge and sing it through several times. That way, the challenges will gradually be resolved.

Achieving a Balance

Working to resolve technical challenges will be tiring on the voice, and must not be overdone. Rest is important after exercise. Some singers will find few technical challenges, depending upon the repertoire they are learning. They may have to work to resolve shortcomings in other areas. A balance must be achieved in consultation with the teacher.

Suggested Warm-Up Routine

Chapter 6

A warm-up routine should be viewed as a "wake-up" call for the muscles used in singing. They will then be ready for the work ahead. An effective warm-up routine should commence with non-vocal physical activities to prepare the muscular systems for work. These should be followed by voiced exercises designed by the teacher to meet the individual needs of the student, pertinent to their stage of development.

Non-Vocal Physical Activities:

Retraction Exercise

(See The Essential Anatomy, Chapter 3, Making Sound – The larynx, The False Vocal Folds)

Exercise:

Laugh silently and with energy for 10 seconds.

Focus on the muscular work involved without the distraction of sound. Be aware of the muscular activity involved in the throat in order to keep the false vocal folds out of the way!

Learning by the feel of this activity rather than by the sound produced will help you gain better control over retraction.

Muscular Support Exercises For Head and Neck Anchoring (all to be done silently): ***(See The Essential Anatomy, Chapter 3, Making Sound – The Larynx, Component Parts of the Larynx)***

These focus on particular muscle groups which support the larynx and the breathing mechanism.

Exercise 1:
Place one hand around the lower neck, with the tip of a finger between the teeth.

Slowly suck on the finger (like a straw in a milkshake!). Observe the muscular contraction in the neck.

Applying slight pressure on the forehead will also engage the neck muscles.

Exercise 2:
Leaving one hand on the lower neck, place the other on the forehead and press slightly; then release. Repeat this several times.

You will feel the neck muscles contracting and relaxing. The contraction of these muscles is very necessary for rising scales and high notes.

Exercise 3:
Imagine being surprised or shocked suddenly and silently! Observe where the work is being done in the body (the abdominals, the back, the sides and in the neck).

The vocal folds close firmly if the action is silent.

Repeat this several times, fully relaxing between each one.

Thyroid Tilt Exercise
(See The Essential Anatomy, Chapter 3, Making Sound – The Larynx, Component Parts of the Larynx; Voice Qualities)

Exercise:
Think of a happy cry and pitch a high note mentally. Silently 'miaouw' repeatedly. Relax in between each one. This is exercising your tilt.

The thyroid part of the larynx has to tilt in order to make our singing sweet, with a freedom, and will help natural vibrato. You may feel the tilt if you wish by placing a finger on the Adam's Apple.

Tilting the thyroid helps you to move more easily into the upper range of the voice.

Breath Support System Activity
(See The Essential Anatomy, Chapter 2, Breathing – Breath Support)

Exercise:
Make the sound Ssshh.......Ssshh.......Ssshh with a vigorous exhalation. Let go and allow the recoil breath after each one; this will feel like a sharp, involuntary intake of air.

Observe the level of effort in the body; the muscles of the Breath Support System are activated quite naturally.

Voiced Physical Activities

Sirening

Exercise:
Say the word "sing" making sure the "ng" is prolonged. The "i" vowel of "sing" raises the larynx in preparation for accessing the higher notes.

Select a note in the middle voice comfort zone and gently slide upwards and downwards, maintaining the "ng" throughout the range. The siren should never be loud.

Notice where the tongue is positioned when forming the "ng": the tip of the tongue is placed behind the lower front teeth, whilst the back of the tongue is raised. This allows maximum freedom for the larynx to rise and fall without any interference from the tongue. It is important to realise that an "ng" will always be nasal in tone.
Breath Support System Activity

(See The Essential Anatomy, Chapter 2, Breathing – Breath Support)

Exercise:
Make a prolonged "VVV" sound with a vigorous exhalation. Let go and allow the recoil of breath between each one; this will feel like a sharp, involuntary intake of air.

Observe the level of effort in the body; the muscles of the breath support system are activated quite naturally. The true vocal folds within the larynx are vibrating but not fully closing.

This is a very safe way for the true vocal folds to prepare for work.

Further singing exercises may be devised by the teacher pertinent to the stage of the singer's development, as an extension of the work already outlined previously in this section and in the ***Making Music*** section.

Further Training Exercises

Chapter Seven

The previous chapters in this section have been dealing with basic training which forms the foundation of good singing. In this chapter, the exercises are designed to move the singer onto a more advanced level.

Sustained Breathing – Three Blind Mice

These exercises are designed to teach the singer to develop the capacity for singing longer phrases. They also connect the clarity of speech to singing.

Exercise:
Sing the phrase clearly and slowly on one sustained breath. The exercises rise chromatically within a comfortable range for the voice. You can select the starting note to suit the voice.

Once exercise 1 is comfortably mastered, move on to exercises 2 and 3 as written below.

Each exercise should be done on one sustained breath.

Exercise 1

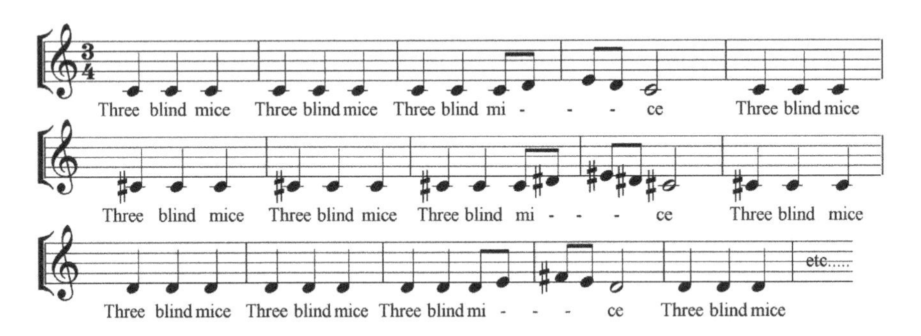

Exercise 2

Exercise 3

Agility Exercises

Vocal music of the Baroque, Classical and Romantic periods ***(See Appendix, Song Genres and Styles)*** requires the singer to move through fast moving passages of notes, over a wide range, with accuracy. Each note must be heard clearly, but not stand out from the phrase. The notes should not be staccato unless indicated in the score.

Exercise:
Sing these phrases smoothly and rapidly, on one breath, in a legato line. No breath should escape between each note.

Interval Exercises to Iron Out Transitions

Exercise 1

Exercise 2

Exercise 3

Exercise 4

These exercises require sustained breath support and train the larynx to change position by small degrees so that there is no audible gear change from the low to the middle voice. They also equalise the upper and lower notes of the scale as they build strength and stamina into the voice.

Exercise:
The following exercises rise by semitones, returning to the original note.

The first series in exercise 1 is suitable for young singers, or those whose stamina is not developed. The second series in exercise 2 is for more advanced singers who have the stamina to sustain the breath over the octave.

For girls and boys with unbroken voices, take the exercise sequence initially from the bottom A of the voice. The highest note of the sequence should be an Eb at the upper end of the range.

For boys with newly broken voices, start on a comfortable low note, then go no higher than the D above middle C.

For adult singers, explore the comfortable range of the voice as it exists, and work to extend this without forcing the voice.

Exercise 1

Exercise 2

SECTION FOUR
The Developing Voice

CHAPTER ONE
Babyhood to Adulthood... and Beyond!

CHAPTER TWO
The Classification of Voices

Babyhood to Adulthood … and beyond!

Chapter One

The voice is in a state of constant change throughout life. The voice passes through various stages, due to physiological changes in the body as we get older. The sounds made by a baby, toddler, child, and adolescent all have their own characteristics, and these are further defined by gender, inherited attributes, native language and dialect. You need to be able to recognise the condition and stage of development of the vocal mechanism by the sounds which your student produces.

There is no point at which a voice settles into a finished product. You should always keep working at technique. Even the adult voice passes through its own stages. It is important that you do not recommend repertoire which is too heavy, in volume or range, for a voice at its particular stage of development. Proper training will keep the singer active and ever-developing.

Song choices should also reflect the emotional range of your student. Giving a 10 year old a song such as "Hello Young Lovers" from "The King and I" is not emotionally appropriate, even though the technical demands of that song may be reasonable for a singer of that age. Giving your student a song which they are not emotionally ready to understand may inhibit their development as a performer and communicator.

The stages of development could fall into the following age ranges:

baby/toddler (from birth to approximately age 4)
childhood (5 to 8 years)
pre-puberty (9 to 11 years)
puberty (12 to 15 years)
adolescence (16 to 19 years)
young adulthood (20 to 30 years)
later adulthood (30 to 50 years)
the ageing voice (50 onwards)

Baby/Toddler (from birth to approximately age 4)

From the moment of birth, healthy babies use the larynx and lungs in a vigorous reflex action which is entirely safe. Babies can cry loudly for extended periods of time with no damage to the voice, because of the way they support the breath. Just observe the work in the abdomen when a baby is in full cry! Re-discovering the link between breath support and the larynx, which is so natural to a baby, is fundamental to vocal health in later life.

The larynx in babies sits high in the throat. It is very small with short vocal folds. The cartilages are soft. The noises produced are high in pitch, can be very loud, but lack wide variation of tone.

Babies then go on to amuse themselves by exploring the range of sounds they hear in their environment. Adults encourage this by using a special language for babies, with cooing, exaggerated pitch changes and simplified words. Babies respond by imitating these sounds and begin to gurgle tunes. They experiment with pitch, volume and length of phrase. A sense of enjoyment and play arises from the sheer physical act of making these sounds. This is so often lost when the teaching of singing becomes formalised.

At this stage, gentle lullabies and nursery rhymes sung by their parents and older children will help to develop a baby's musical ear.

Childhood (age range 5 to 8 years)

As the baby moves into childhood, the larynx begins to grow and to drop lower in the throat. The increase in the length of the pharynx allows for a wider variation of tone, and the increasing length of the vocal folds allows for a greater variety of pitch.

It is interesting to note that the vocal folds in boys tend to grow at a faster rate than in girls. Despite the slightly larger vocal folds, girls and boys speak at around the same pitch, but girls tend develop a wider singing range earlier.

Children in this age range will develop naturally by singing in groups. They need to explore their voices to discover pitch, and they learn to sing in tune more readily by listening to others in their group. At this stage, you should not insist too much upon accuracy of pitch or memory of words if this will interfere with the overall enjoyment of the experience.

The type of songs which children of this age enjoy, and respond well to, are nursery rhymes and songs with accompanying actions and repetition.

Pre-puberty (9 to 11 years)

An ideal age for a child to begin individual singing lessons would be about 9 years. It is advisable that children should not sing too high in their range nor too loudly for extended periods of time.

Your choice of repertoire is very important and should be influenced by the child's musical experience so far, which can vary greatly from child to child. The sense of enjoyment should not be lost in these early singing lessons, so find out what type of music the child likes, and build up a repertoire with this in mind. Children of this age respond well to songs which tell a story, animal songs, character songs, and comedy songs.

Generally, a child will learn the words of a song more quickly than the tune. They will also learn more easily through the process of imitation. To this end, you should sing the tune to the child rather than just play it on an instrument, and continue to sing along with the child as he or she learns the song. You can then stop singing along when the child feels more confident.

A well-structured programme of training can produce very gratifying standards of achievement in this age group.

Puberty (12 to 15 years)

The onset of puberty generally occurs earlier in girls than in boys, but most youngsters fall into the 12 to 15 age range. This stage of development triggers a series of growth spurts followed by recovery periods. The development is not regular. An increase in hormonal levels produces an increased growth in the body as a whole, including the larynx, with resultant changes in the voice.

This age range will be enthusiastic about current popular music, a lot of which is not suitable for the developing voice. If you can find the right popular song, which sits comfortably in your student's vocal range, this will maintain their interest. These songs can be taught alongside classical songs and songs from musical theatre.

Boys' Voices

The vocal changes are most noticeable in boys. The larynx grows so large that it can be seen moving in the throat. It is commonly called the "Adam's Apple". The vocal folds become longer and increase in muscle mass, with a consequent lowering of range of pitch. The pharynx becomes longer and wider, adding depth of resonance to the voice.

Boys may try to speak and sing using the muscle memory of their pre-pubescent, unchanged voice. This no longer works, resulting in squeaks and "breaks". New habits need to be developed to allow the fast-developing instrument to function properly.

At this stage, it is important for the teacher to realise that although vocal stability is difficult to control, this process of vocal change is entirely natural. It is also important that a boy should continue singing throughout this period of vocal change. A boy is not told to stop playing football or give up all sports while going through the physical changes of puberty. In the same way, exercising the voice by singing will help it to grow and be strong.

You should be aware that any of the following may happen:

1. In ideal circumstances, the pitch range of the voice lowers steadily without any break and remains intact.
2. In extreme circumstances, the boy wakes up one morning with a completely different voice functioning in a lower register, with access to a much weaker upper voice.
3. What is almost certain to happen is that there will be a definite change of register in the voice, with a limited thick fold sound of approximately one octave below the change, and an easier falsetto range above.

The job of the teacher should be to develop the middle range of the changed voice and extend this range both up and down the scale.

Repertoire choices become considerably limited, due to the loss of range, but you should select songs, or parts of songs, which cover the range at which the voice is working easily. A boy should not be made to continue to sing as a treble or alto beyond a reasonable period after the voice begins to show change. This may cause conflict, undue strain and slow down the development of the adult voice.

A counter-tenor voice ***(See Chapter 2 of this Section, The Classification of Voices)*** may be developed, but this will be at the expense of the emerging tenor, baritone or bass voice. It is a matter of choice as to which type of voice you wish to develop through training.

Girls' Voices

The vocal change in a girl's voice is generally less dramatic, and begins earlier. A noticeable breathiness often appears, due to the temporary inability of the vocal folds to close fully. This is because of the accelerated growth process occurring in puberty. As with boys, the vocal folds thicken, and there may be evidence of register changes, or transitions. These give easier access to the lower notes in some girls' voices.

Teachers and singers have even referred to having different "voices" (head or chest) on either side of these gear changes or transitions. In truth, there is only one voice. The singer must learn to control the transitions by controlling the relative thickness of the vocal folds and the position of the larynx in the throat. Sirening is a great help here. ***(See Training the Singing Voice, Chapter 6, Suggested Warm-up Routine, Sirening)***

The notion of a "head" or "chest" voice arises from the sensations of resonance which are felt in these areas on varying pitches. The teacher must strive to mix these resonances and sensations so that the tone quality is balanced throughout the range. This will also help to smooth out any gear changes. ***(See The Essential Anatomy, Chapter 4, Modifying Sound – The Resonators, The Nose and Head Sinuses; The Chest)***

The transition from one area of the voice to another (from low to middle to high ranges) is called a register change. The notes upon which the register change occurs is called the "passaggio". Notes in the "passaggio" often feel weaker but should never be forced. If force is used moving from a lower to a higher register, the transition into the next register will not happen. The voice will sound driven and pushed. This is very unhealthy for the voice and can build up long term problems. Some people mistake this for belt quality, which it is not.

In this phase of vocal change, it is important not to be quick to categorise the voice as either a soprano, mezzo-soprano or contralto. You should listen to the tonal quality of the voice and work on a variety of repertoire allowing the voice to settle into its preferred range in its own time.

Throughout the physical changes of puberty, a guiding principal of exercises for boys and girls alike should be the siren ("ng"), as well as descending scale work. Girls at this age should be discouraged from over-developing the lower range of their voice. This sound may be enjoyable and easy to make, but does not carry through to higher pitches with ease. They should work on the upper, middle and lower parts of the voice equally, to ensure the muscular development of all parts of the voice.

Adolescence (16 to 19 years)
At this stage of development, the voice usually has gone through the most extreme changes that it will ever experience. This phase is where stamina and consolidation should be the focal points of training.

In some cases, the voice can appear to be quite settled, but don't be tempted to burden the voice with repertoire which is extreme in range and dramatic content. It is an excellent time to be building in agility and length of phrase.

The choice of repertoire should be challenging, both technically and emotionally, but do keep within your student's capabilities as you try to extend them. You can also challenge students by introducing genres and styles which they would not ordinarily have considered for themselves.

For the classical repertoire, the early composers such as Purcell, Bach, Handel, Haydn and Mozart provide ideal songs for the adolescent voice. For musical theatre and more popular music, be careful about the range of the song, especially for boys' voices. You should be able to find songs in a variety of keys to suit the abilities of your students. ***(See Appendix, Song Genres and Styles)***

When choosing repertoire, be sure that the accompaniment is not too overpowering for the voice. It can be discouraging for a young singer to feel swamped by the density of the accompaniment so that they strain to be heard.

Young Adulthood (20 to 30 years)
This is the period of life when much more vigorous training of the singing voice can be undertaken. The pharynx has developed to its full length and width, and the cartilage systems with their accompanying musculature have now reached their full size.

The vocal folds have also reached their full length, and the muscles within them are now ready to take on harder work. The breath support system has now settled and can be worked upon to produce longer phrases and louder dynamics.

Everything is now in place for improving tonal quality and extending the range of the voice. It should be remembered that from the age of 25 the soft cartilages of the larynx begin to harden and become more dense. This is the first step of the aging process of the voice.

Later Adulthood (30 to 50 years)

At this stage of life, the singer should be able to access abundant stamina and vocal flexibility. The tone is at its peak of potential and the voice should be able to work with a wide variety of dynamic and energy. The voice is also capable of sustaining longer periods of higher tessitura and louder dynamics without strain.

The teacher should feel confident in working with voices in this age range as they should be fully settled into voice type and capable of working hard. The singer is also of an age where the emotional and intellectual life is flourishing, and so will be capable of a wide range of styles and musical challenge.

The Ageing Voice (50 onwards)

Please remember that the ageing process of the voice commences at about age 25, when the soft cartilages of the larynx begin to harden and become more dense. The aging process can inhibit the function of the larynx, affecting flexibility, pitch and tonal quality. This can be counteracted by a greater input from the muscles which control the movement of the larynx.

Constant maintenance in the form of proper exercise will ensure that the voice will function at its best. There is no reason why the voice should sound 'old'. Deterioration of muscular function is the true cause of a voice which sounds 'old'. Keep singing, as long as you are prepared to practise!

The Classification of Voices

Chapter 2

The section on The Developing Voice should conclude with a consideration of the standard classification of voices. SATB (soprano, alto, tenor, bass) is a concept designed to facilitate choral and part-singing. Sometimes, singers are trained into these categories without much consideration as to where the voice feels most comfortable when singing.

Certain voices are happier with higher pitches, and others enjoy working with lower ones. The timbre of the voice can be misleading, especially in young voices. For example, a young baritone can sound like a tenor. Asking them to sing the tenor line in a choral group can strain their voice, when it would be better for them to sing the bass line.

With young voices in particular, it is important not to pigeon-hole them too soon into these limiting categories. For example, a girl with a thin timbre to her voice is not necessarily a soprano. She may be more comfortable in the middle and low range of the voice and would be more suited to singing the alto line. It is always preferable to allow the voice to explore and discover its own natural tessitura.

Some of the standard SATB repertoire is unsuitable for the vocal abilities of adolescents, except for those girls who remain sopranos throughout puberty. For the other voices, the range of pitch within the SATB categories can often put too much strain on the developing voice. Choice of choral repertoire for young singers is fundamentally important to their vocal and musical development.

The SATB system shows its limitations when you consider the sub-divisions which exist within the voice types.

The soprano may be the highest of the female voices, but there are many different types of soprano. The lighter types of soprano have agility (coloratura) with a wide vocal range and ease at the top of the voice. These are categorised as light and lyric sopranos. The heavier, darker voices are called "spinto," and dramatic sopranos, but these also have good top notes.

The mezzo-soprano voice may have the same range of notes as the soprano, but feels more comfortable singing in the middle and lower range of the voice. Often the sound is darker and warmer than the soprano, and can also fall into coloratura and dramatic categories.

The lowest female voice is the contralto, which is dark and full in tone and lies comfortably in the lower register. Often the higher notes are limited in this type of voice. A true contralto voice is quite rare.

The male voice which sings in the same general range as the lower female voices is called the counter-tenor, male alto or haute-contre. This type of voice emerges after puberty, has a distinctive timbre which is unlike the female voices, and often sings a similar repertoire of early music. It is usually a form of developed falsetto.

The tenor carries the middle voice sound up the scale into a higher register without changing to falsetto. There are as many subdivisions of tenor as there are for soprano: light, lyric, spinto, dramatic, and helden or heroic, all indicating differences in vocal weight and colour.

The baritone is the most common of male voices, and indicates a vocal colour more than a range. Many baritones can access both bass and tenor notes, but feel comfortable in the middle range of the voice. Again, there can be high, light, lyric and dramatic classifications of the baritone voice.

The bass is the lowest of the male voices, with dark tone and especial strength at the bottom end of the range. They are not usually expected to sing high notes, but often can produce them easily. True basses, like true contraltos, are rare.

Some points to consider when categorising a voice are:
the range of notes is not the only indicator of voice type
the foremost consideration should be where the voice sits most comfortably in the range, not what notes the singer can access
a dark timbre does not mean that the voice is most comfortable in the lower range
a light timbre does not mean that the voice is comfortable in the higher range

It is especially difficult to categorise a young singer in the adolescent stage of development. It becomes easier when the voice grows into the young adult stage and begins to settle down. As the singer grows into the young adult stage, more specific training can direct the voice into a category appropriate to its inherent characteristics. This type of training should not occur too early in the developmental process.

SECTION FIVE

Practical Singing for all Musicians

CHAPTER ONE
Singing is the Basis of all Musicianship

CHAPTER TWO
Aural Training - Using Your Ears to Find Your Voice

CHAPTER THREE
A Practical Approach to Aural Training

CHAPTER FOUR
Practical Singing for Examinations

Singing is the Basis of all Musicianship

Chapter One

Previous sections explored the mechanics and function of the voice and how to train it effectively. This section shows how singing may be used to develop the wider skills of general musicianship.

Many of the practical exercises contained in this section may be used with equal success either when teaching groups or individuals. Instrumentalists as well as singers will benefit from using these exercises to improve aural and rhythm skills.

The human voice is the primal musical instrument. All other instruments are external and manufactured. Whether alone or combined with other voices, it can carry melody, emotion and meaning. For this reason, all musicians should be encouraged, from the beginning of training, to use the singing voice.

Other instruments were invented to accompany this fundamental experience, and have evolved into powerful means of musical expression, so that they now stand on their own merits. Nevertheless, terms such as "making the instrument sing" still show that fundamental connection.

There is a difference between playing a composition mechanically and playing it as a piece of communicated music. That difference resides in the skill of inward singing, an act of imagination where the music is personalised and becomes an outward expression. The melody, emotion and meaning inherent in the human voice can thus be transferred to the instrument.

The following is an exercise for an instrumentalist.

Exercise:
Inward singing can be developed through the following:
Select a musical phrase from a composition which you are currently studying. Sing it aloud (either sirening or on a vowel)

Imagine singing the phrase, and then sing that phrase silently whilst playing it on your instrument.

(See Training the Singing Voice , Chapter 6 Suggested Warm-Up Routine, Sirening)

This exercise should be repeated at regular intervals to encourage the practice of inward singing to become habitual. Phrasing, line and legato all emerge through inward singing.

The instrumentalist needs this skill in order to cross the barrier from technical exercise to living music. Mastering this skill will produce a communicated outward performance. We inwardly sing the music we hear in order to learn it, so this skill also helps in memorising music.

Aural Training – Using Your Ears to Find Your Voice

Chapter Two

Speaking and Singing are Learned Skills

We are born with all the physical equipment necessary for speaking and singing, but we have to learn how to use it. We do this through hearing.

We learn to speak by hearing others do it – by hearing our parents and those around us, whilst we are growing up. We acquire their vocal habits in the process. The most obvious of these habits is accent. It would be unusual for a child born in Manchester to begin speaking with a South London accent.

There are other factors. For example, if a parent's speech is very nasal, we are likely to sound nasal also. ***(See Section 10, Troubleshooting, Nasality)*** This characteristic of imitating those we hear around us is very strong. Often, if we hear a daughter on the telephone, we may mistake her for her mother. The same can also be true with a father, son or brother.

Imitating what we hear is a fundamental ability which you can draw upon to develop pitch recognition and rhythm in your own teaching.

Recognising Pitch

It is important to establish as early as possible whether the singer can recognise pitch. There are a very small number of people who cannot do this, and they are the truly tone-deaf. ***(See Training the Singing Voice, Chapter 4, What Is Good Singing, The Singing is in Tune)***

Exercise:
Play middle C on an instrument followed by the E a third above.
You can play this sequence several times over, making sure that your student identifies note 1 (C) followed by note 2 (E).
1. Ask your student whether they have noticed a difference in pitch.
2. Ask your student to identify the higher pitch (note 1 or note 2?).

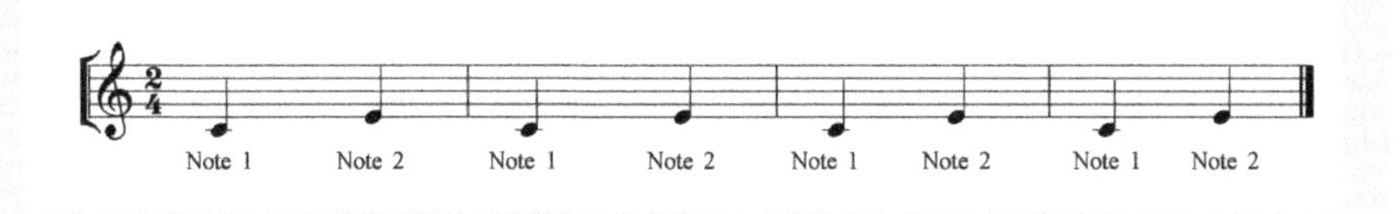

If your student can recognise that there is a difference in pitch, and that one note is higher than the other, it indicates that their ear is not faulty and, therefore, trainable.

Exercise:
The exercise may be repeated using different pitches and different intervals, both wide and narrow.

Each time, ask your student to identify which note is higher, or lower, in pitch.

Listening is Different from Hearing

Listening is different from the simple act of hearing. Hearing is something we do naturally, even involuntarily, whereas we have to learn how to listen. The brain is engaged when we listen; it analyses and selects the input. We call this "developing the ear", and repetition plays an important part in this process.

Through repetition, the student comes to recognise pitch, intervals, rhythm and harmony, while at the same time developing the memory. These are the building blocks of musicianship and this whole process is aural training.

Examination of aural training requires that you put into sound what has been heard by the ears and understood by the brain. In other words, you have to sing!

Singing is at the heart of developing aural skills, and aural skills improve greatly through singing. Instrumentalists will benefit by vocalising phrases from the pieces they are learning, as singing is the basis of all musicianship and at the heart of developing aural skills.

A basic understanding of how the voice works will make for more confident students. Teachers with this knowledge can enable their students to enjoy their aural work and build up these essential skills which will make them better, all-round musicians.

Repeating What you Hear

The next step is that your student should sing or hum a note which they hear, demonstrating that they can not only recognise a pitch, but can also reproduce it. This activity should be fun for the student.

Through this process the teacher will begin to learn about the student's voice, such as the range in which it is most comfortable, before further training is undertaken.

Exercise:
Play a series of different notes on the instrument.

The student repeats the notes by sirening ("ng") or singing on a vowel in response.

If the student cannot sing the note which is played, then strategies must be developed to enable them to do so. If they can recognise differences in pitch as shown by the previous activity, the problem does not lie in the ear.

From your reading of The Essential Anatomy section, you will know that there are two main elements governing pitch in singing:

the position of the larynx in the throat, and
muscular activity in the breath support system.
(See Training the Singing Voice, Chapter 1, Relating Sound to the Anatomy, Pitch)

Finding a note in the singing voice entails experimenting in both these areas.

Your student should siren (the "ng" sound) up and down; this encourages the larynx to slide up and down in the throat. When the student reaches the note played, your finger stops moving.

Exercise 1:
Play or sing the notes on the stave below.

Use your index finger to help your student to visualise the changing pitch. You can then control the range of the siren, narrowing it down until it settles on the note played.

Repetition of this exercise will gradually enable the student to remember the feeling associated with the pitch.

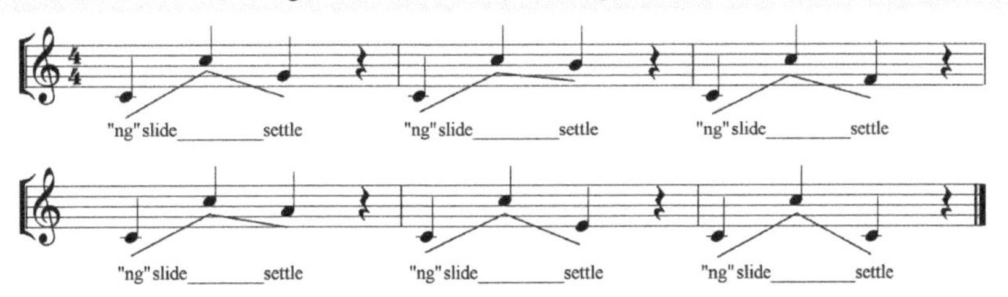

This exercise can be repeated using the "VVV" sound. This sound activates the breathing and support system and reinforces the relationship between air pressure and pitch.

Exercise 2:
Sing or play the notes below on the instrument of choice.

Use your index finger to help your student to visualise the changing pitch. You can then control the range of the "VVV" slide, narrowing it down until it settles on the note played.

Repetition of this exercise will gradually enable the student to remember the feeling associated with the pitch.

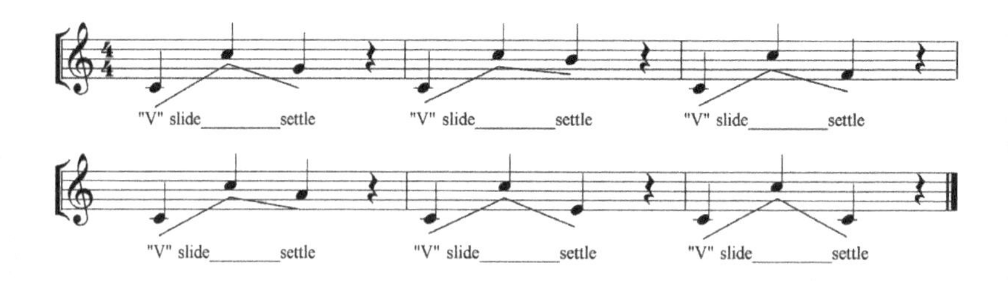

Recognising intervals

The next step in aural training is to recognise intervals and to sing them.

Exercise:
Sing or play the sequence of notes below on the instrument of choice.

Ask your student to repeat the sequence, firstly on "ng" (siren) sliding from the first note to the next.

Then sing the sequence using the numbers.

Echo Response to a Voice

Imitation is a powerful tool, so the student will learn by imitating the teacher. Echo singing should be practised in two ways : responding to a voice, then responding to an instrument.

Exercise:

Responding to a singing voice:

Sing short phrases using the number of the notes in the octave.

Ask your student to repeat this, also using the numbers of the notes.

You can develop this exercise by using a variety keys and changing the note sequences.

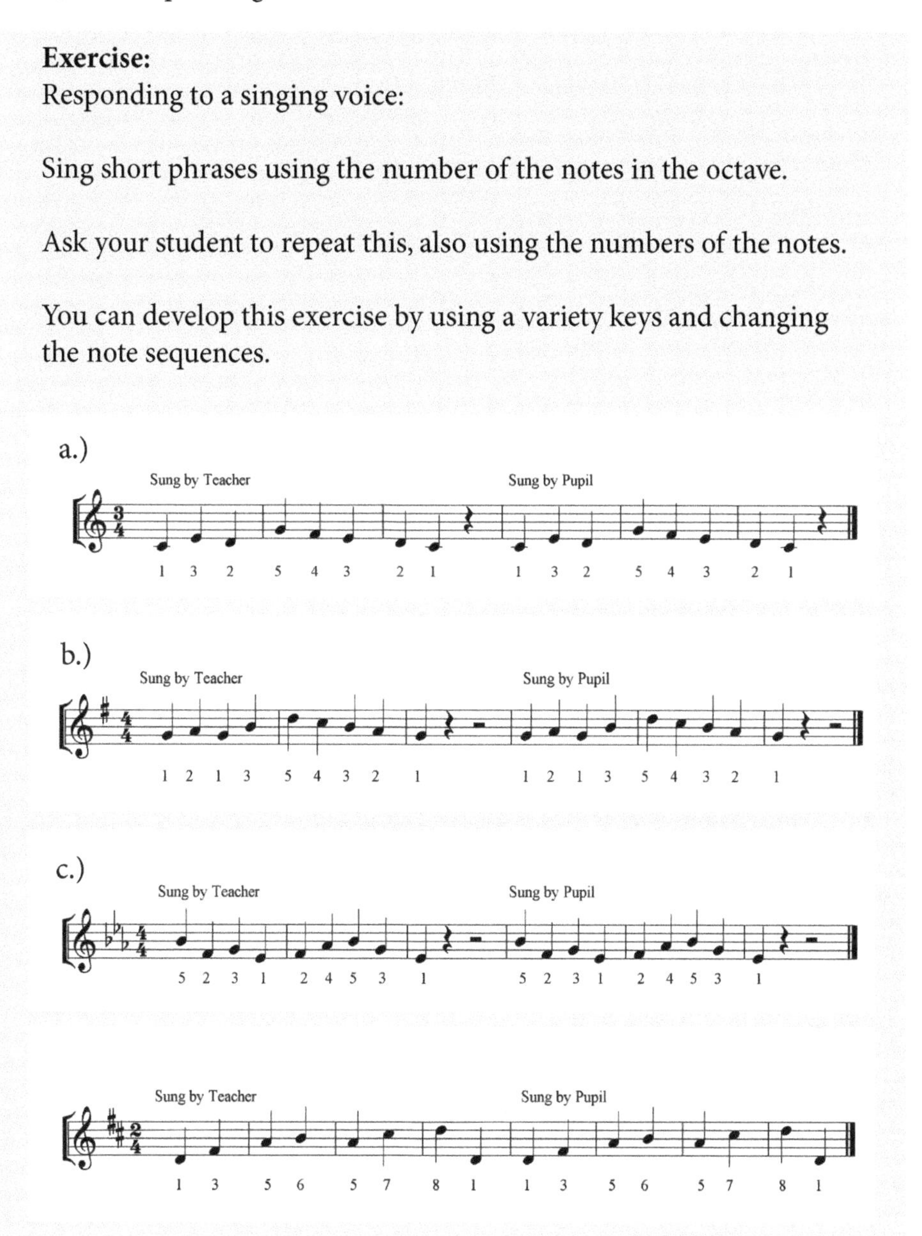

Echo response to an instrument

This time, your student should echo the note played on an instrument.

Exercise:
Responding to an instrument:

Play the tune on an instrument. Ask your student to repeat the note, first
a) by using "ng" (siren), then
b) by using the numbered notes within an octave.

This will show that your student can recognise the intervals.

You can develop this exercise by using a variety keys and changing the note sequences.

a.)

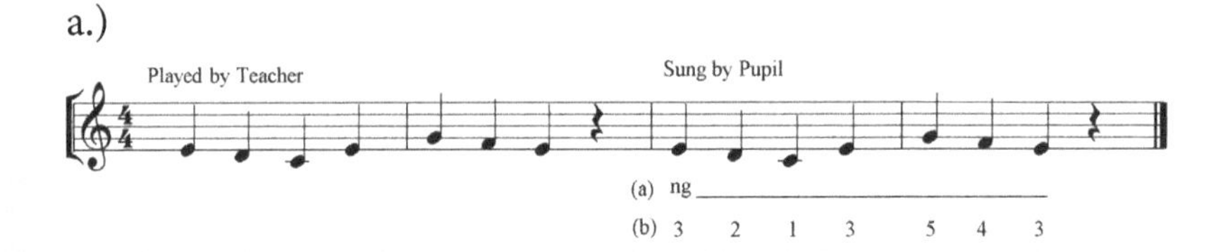

b.)

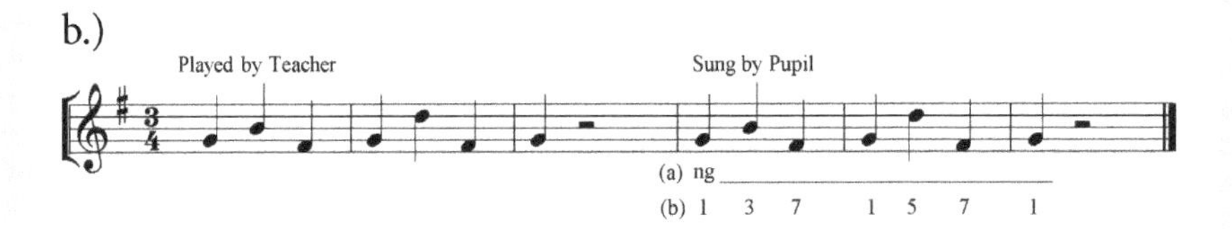

c.)

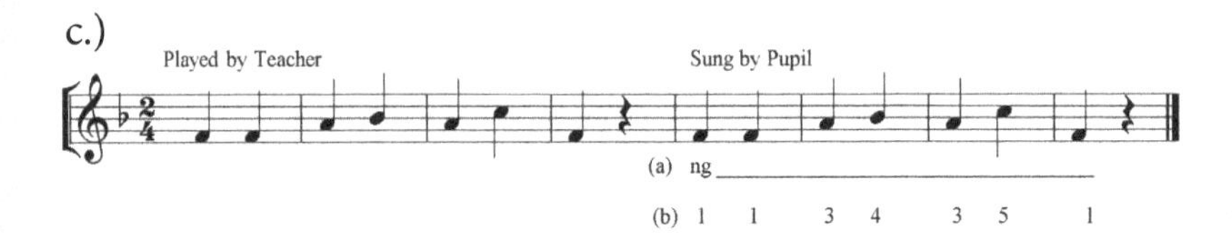

d.)

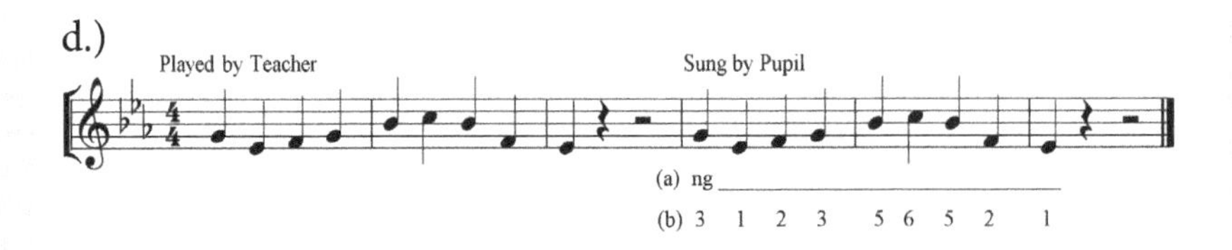

Recognising Rhythm

An essential part of aural training is the ability to recognise rhythm. All of the above exercises have purposely been notated using one crotchet per syllable. This should encourage your student to build up some confidence in recognising pitch and in singing intervals.

Now it becomes important to add rhythm to the notated intervals to make your student aware of the main pulses of 2 and 3 time.

Exercise:
Clap the rhythm, or play the note sequences on an instrument.

Ask your student to clap the rhythm back to you.

Singing with Rhythm

Now that your student has shown that they can recognise patterns of rhythm, they can add their singing voice to the rhythm.

Exercise:

Play and sing the note sequence, using the numbers for each note.

Ask your student to sing the sequence back to you, also using the numbers.

Notice that the melody remains the same although the rhythmic patterns change for each exercise.

You may use the above examples as a springboard for developing your own particular exercises, tailored to the individual needs of your students. Using these exercises will ensure that your student become used to singing as part of their general musical training.

A Practical Approach to Aural Training

Chapter Three

There are many ways of approaching aural training. Whatever the approach, it needs to be a frequent part of the training for all musicians, and not just preparing for examinations. The following suggestions are designed to give you some practical ideas, so that you may go on to develop further methods of your own.

Regular Group Aural Classes

The life of an instrumentalist can be a solitary one! So much practising has to be done alone. By holding regular group classes where your students can learn together, they should not feel so isolated, and can have a sociable time with other learners.

A regular group class will complement the one-to-one lessons, and great strides can be made in aural proficiency. You are also saved the burden of repeating the material over and over to each separate student. A group class can produce a little healthy competition. Such a class is cost-effective for students and parents, and will give you, as teachers, variety in your work.

You can step out of that formal mode every now and then and just enjoy making music with your students. It is a less stressful environment and more fun for all!

Sing Group Songs in Unison

To complement a regular group aural class, consider having a group singing class, particularly if you are teaching within a school. This can also open the way for an occasional concert.

Most youngsters like to listen to the pop music of the day, so give them a good quality pop song to sing. Allow them freedom within that style, as it will help their musical ear to develop.

Do the same with a musical theatre song, and then tackle a classical song, all in the same session. Your students will enjoy the opportunity of making a variety of music together, and will enjoy their one-to-one lessons all the more. Here are a few examples from different genres which have always proved to be enjoyable. ***(See Appendix, Song Genres and Styles)***

Folk: My Bonny Lies Over the Ocean (anon)
Classical: Caro Mio Ben (Giordano)
Musical Theatre: Lullaby of Broadway (Warren)
Pop: The Greatest Love of All (Masser)

As we have discussed earlier, singing will enhance instrumental playing and you may have a few instrumentalists who would like to take the occasional Grade Exam in Singing. It is not unreasonable for instrumental teachers to nurture singing in their students, and even encourage them to take a grade exam in singing. The information in this book provides you with a sound, basic understanding of singing to enhance your teaching in this area.

Sing 2- and 3-Part Songs

Learning to sing in harmony can be an exciting and fulfilling way to develop aural skills. Select songs from a wide variety of styles, such as folk, classical, musical theatre and pop. If the songs are not readily available as 2– and 3–part harmony, then take a tune & create harmony parts yourself. ***(See Appendix, Song Genres and Styles)***

Once one part has been learned, your students should swap parts. This broadens their experience of melody and harmony in a simple context. This is also good preparation for having to recognise another part, and to sing either the top part or lower part as is required in some examination aural tests.

There are many established arrangements of 2- and 3-part songs, which are easily available. Here are some suggestions, all of which are interchangeable with voices for the purposes of building those aural skills:

Evening Prayer (from 'Hansel and Gretel') by Humperdinck
Lovely Peace (from 'Judas Maccabaeus') by Handel
Come, Ever-Smiling Liberty (from 'Judas Maccabaeus') by Handel
Panis Angelicus by Cesar Franck
Ave Verum Corpus (duet version) by Mozart
You're Just In Love (from 'Call Me Madam') by Irving Berlin
Play A Simple Melody (from 'Watch Your Step') by Irving Berlin
I Know Him So Well (from 'Chess') by Andersson, Rice & Ulvaeus

(See Appendix, Song Genres and Styles)
For the adventurous, why not even attempt the "Who Will Buy?" sextet from 'Oliver' by Lionel Bart and "Skid Row" from "The Little Shop of Horrors" by Alan Menken.

When your students have grasped the principles of singing in harmony, they could be encouraged to harmonise sections of those group songs by ear. This will really improve their aural skills and introduce them to improvisation.

For those more advanced students who may be considering the higher levels of examination, you may wish to concentrate on classical 4-part pieces, such as the Bach Chorales.

Sing Phrases from Exam Pieces.
In order to develop the process of singing inwardly, ask your student to prepare a phrase or two from their instrumental exam pieces. At their next lesson, ask them to sing them to you.

When they have sung the phrase to you, ask them why they chose that phrase to sing. Ask them about the shape of the phrase, the dynamics (crescendo and diminuendo), the tonality (major? minor?), the character (happy? sad?), the tempo. This will give you an idea of how they are thinking musically.

Your student can then experiment with the sung phrase, altering any or all of the above. They should observe how these changes affect the nature of the music. This experimenting will help your student to understand that they have a choice in the way they can interpret a phrase. This is why no two performances are ever identical, and these subtle differences keep the music fresh and alive.

Your student can then play the phrase on their instrument, keeping the shape and dynamic that they discovered through their singing of it. Continue to encourage your students to sing inwardly what they are playing outwardly; it helps them develop as all-round musicians.

Use Books and CDs on Aural Training
It is strongly recommended that you obtain resources to help structure your teaching of aural work. There are many on the market, such as 'Aural Training In Practice' with accompanying CDs, published by the ABRSM.

They provide background notes to guide you through the entire aural part of each exam.

Look for resources which contain practice exercises, and which would work well in a group situation as well as in individual lessons. If your students are preparing for grade examinations or GCSE and A level, they are more likely to gain higher marks in the aural sections of their exams if you work systematically through these exercises with them.

It is very easy to leave aural preparation for an examination until the last few weeks, but this is not a good idea. Aural training needs to be at the heart of our musical development, so it must be ongoing, not just left until the last minute. Even if your student does not wish to enter for an examination, the skills developed through the exercises in these books will complement their training as musicians.

Practical Singing for Examinations

Chapter Four

Since examinations have already been mentioned several times in this section, now would be a good time to talk about them in some detail. There are many boards which offer graded examinations. You should look through the various syllabuses and decide which best suits you and your student's requirements.

The Role of Examinations

Examinations are a valuable means of establishing a consistent level by which achievement may be measured. They are a good monitoring device to show your student's progress and development, and the standard is recognised world-wide.

Success in graded examinations provides your student with a strong incentive to continue studying because of pride in achievement and a sense of progress. The syllabus which you choose should provide a good cross-section of repertoire appropriate to your student's musical and technical ability. You can also use material suggested for the examinations as a guideline when selecting repertoire for your students.

Examinations suggest a way of structuring teaching, whilst giving your student the opportunity to perform. Preparation for examinations should promote the general musical development of your student. They can be used as a benchmark of achievement, but not necessarily the only one. Examinations should not be thought of as an end in themselves.

The Necessity of Exams

Besides indicating a level of achievement, the examinations also provide useful feedback in the form of comments from the examiner. This invariably reinforces the role of the teacher, who may find themselves saying the same thing over and over again, but often, the penny only drops when the examiner also offers the same comment.

The deadline of an examination is a goal which serves to focus the mind of your student and reinforces the need for practice. Hopefully, this increased motivation will mean that practice is undertaken on a regular basis.

Coping with the pressure of doing an examination is a valuable learning exercise for your student. It also prepares them for future public performance.

The Purpose of Exams

As has been mentioned earlier, examinations are not just about learning a group of songs and performing them to an acceptable technical standard. The whole musical development of your student is addressed in the process of preparing for an examination.

General musicianship is covered not only by aural work and sight-singing, but in learning the demands imposed by different styles of song. Training the voice to cope with the various demands of different repertoire increases technical skill.

Understanding the songs and communicating them to the examiner is the foundation of performance work. The examination should be approached as a performance in its own right.

The whole of the examination process – learning, understanding, practising, memorising, rehearsing and performing – demands self-discipline, a quality which is valuable in any sphere of achievement.

The Benefit of Exams

By providing a recognised benchmark of achievement, examinations open up a world of progression for the successful candidate. "A" Level Music and University and College entrance requirements value the standards of the higher levels of the Graded Examinations Boards.

Examinations can provide you with a clear way of structuring a learning programme for your student at all levels. There will be enough variety of repertoire to cater to the individual needs of your student, which is a good basis for well-informed teaching. Parents are given a recognised form of quality control with which to monitor their child's progress.

The structure of graded examinations provides you with the early stages of programme planning for a recital. The various sections from which to select repertoire present a range of styles and period, with differing moods and pace. The examination programme should be interesting and varied, as is expected for a recital.

SECTION SIX

Making Music

CHAPTER ONE
Choosing Repertoire

CHAPTER TWO
Putting it all Together

Choosing Repertoire

Chapter One

Getting to Know your Student

Selecting a song for a student is one of the most important things a teacher can do, and must be given very careful consideration. You must get to know your student's voice. This knowledge will emerge through the exercises given in the first part of the lesson.

There is a good range of exercises in the section on Training The Singing Voice. These will give an indication of:
the comfortable range of the voice,
the breadth of dynamic (volume) available without strain,
the natural character of the voice, and
the level of technical control at that point in your student's development.

(See Training The Singing Voice; The Developing Voice, Chapter 1, Babyhood to Adulthood ... and Beyond, and Chapter 2, The Classification of Voices)

In order to maintain your student's interest, it is advisable that you adopt a holistic approach. The voice is not independent of the person; it is a part of our personality. You should begin the process of selecting repertoire in the light of what you know about your student.

What are their interests?
What music do they listen to at home?
Who are their favourite performers?
What do they sing for their own pleasure?
What do they know about different styles of song?

It is helpful to remember that boys and girls tend to be interested in different things, and that a generalised selection of songs for both sexes is not always the best approach to take in order to keep your individual student's interest alive.

Choosing Songs Appropriate to Age

The song choices should reflect the emotional range of your student. Giving a 12 year old a song such as "Hello Young Lovers" from "The King and I" is not emotionally appropriate, even though the technical demands of that song may be reasonable for a singer of that age.

Giving your student a song which they are not emotionally ready to understand may inhibit their development as a performer and communicator. It may be helpful to think of these age groupings when making repertoire choices :

5 – 8 years
9 – 11 years
12 – 15 years
16 – 19 years
20 + years

(See The Developing Voice, Chapter 1, Babyhood to Adulthood … and Beyond, and Chapter 2, The Classification of Voices)

The 5 to 8 year old age range will be stimulated by nursery rhymes and simple character songs, whereas the 9 to 11 age range will have outgrown these. Folk songs which tell a story are a good choice for this group, as are more complex character songs.

The next age ranges will be enthusiastic about current popular music, a lot of which is not suitable for the developing voice. If you can find the right popular song, which sits comfortably in your student's vocal range, this will maintain their interest. These songs can be taught alongside classical songs and songs from musical theatre.

Of course, the choice of repertoire should be challenging, both technically and emotionally, but do keep within your student's capabilities as you try to extend them. You can also challenge students by introducing genres and styles which they would not ordinarily have considered for themselves.

The Importance of Variety

To maintain your student's interest, it is a good idea to have two or three songs in development from the outset of training, even for the complete beginner. An initial choice of song may be a folk song, which would be easy to learn, with simple rhythms and melody.

Folk songs also tend to lie in the middle range of the voice. Once your student has learned the tune and the words, you can begin to work with them on interpreting the song and resolving technical issues.

At this point, another song should be added into the lesson. This could be a lighter character piece, drawn from the musical theatre, commercial pop or even modern Classical genres, according to your student's preferences and tastes.

At a later stage a more challenging song can be introduced, which can be drawn from the traditional Classical genre. These choices will broaden their overall development as musicians, as well as benefit their singing. ***(See Appendix, Song Genres and Styles)***

A range of repertoire can be selected from the syllabuses of the various graded singing examination boards. A broad selection of songs can also be accessed through the ABRSM Songbooks Grades 1 to 5. In doing this, you will be laying the foundations of a varied programme for performances, such as graded singing examinations, school concerts, music festivals, auditions and other presentations before an audience.

Classifying the Repertoire

Vocal music for the solo voice comes in many different forms, from the simplest folk song to the complexities of the twenty-first century art song, with the popular forms of musical theatre, pop and rock along the way. Each makes its own demands on musical and technical ability, and each has a particular type of sound by which it is recognised. For example, it simply does not work to try to sing a rock song in the style of an operatic aria. You need to be able to recognise the genre, style and idiom of any repertoire which you select for your student's, and know how to teach the voice qualities necessary for that piece.

Classifications of types of song are known as "genre". Broadly speaking, the most common genres are :

folk song
classical
musical theatre
jazz and blues
commercial pop
rock

Each of these classifications contains subdivisions, which are known as "style".

Within each genre there is a variety of different styles. In the classical genre, we can see that Baroque, Classical, Romantic and Modern styles of music each have different characteristics and make different demands in performance. For example, there are stylistic differences between 17th, 18th and 19th century works, between Italian Canzona, German Lied, French Mélodie and English Art Song. The portamento of the Italian 19th century romantic song should not be brought to the singing of Bach.

The way in which a song may be performed is referred to as the "idiom". A clear example of this would be the different vocal sound required by a 20th century musical theatre song when compared with a classical contemporary piece.

Songs carry with them a requirement to be performed in a particular way. For example, it is irritating to hear "Can't Help Lovin' Dat Man o' Mine" from "Show Boat", sung as if it were a classical song. It is not! The sentiments contained in it become artificial and insincere if the classical idiom is imposed upon it. Equally, the vibrant jollity of a Music Hall Song needs a sound appropriate to the mood. Adapting the sound of the voice to make it appropriate to the style of the song entails the appropriate use of voice qualities.

It is also possible to take a song from a certain style and present it in a different idiom. A famous example of this would be Ella Fitzgerald, who took the songs of George Gershwin and Cole Porter, and performed them in the idiom of the Jazz genre. She was so successful in this that her performances are now accepted as definitive, and the original idiomatic way of performing these songs has now almost been forgotten.

There is a list of the different genres and some of their relative subdivisions of style in an appendix at the end of this book. ***(See Appendix, Song Genres and Styles)***

Putting It All Together

Chapter Two

Choosing Voice Qualities

As you will know from the sections on The Essential Anatomy and Training the Singing Voice, voice qualities arise naturally from emotion. To choose the appropriate quality, you and your student need to discuss the emotion inherent in the song. Is it happy, sad, angry, excited? Does the rhythm help to define the emotional content?

Broadly speaking, we can identify an emotion with a voice quality. For example, a happy emotion is best conveyed by cry/tilt quality. In reality the song would be performed using a mixture of speech and cry/tilt qualities. It is useful to exaggerate the cry/tilt quality (raised larynx with thyroid tilt) when building the song into the voice. Any difficulties in accessing the higher notes of the song will be greatly reduced by using this quality.

The sound most associated with classical singing is produced by lowering the larynx and tilting the thyroid cartilage. This is called sob/tilt quality. The sound is gentle, soft grained, and darker in timbre. This means that in order to project, it has to be mixed with speech quality, and by adding twang resonance. The emotion which produces pure sob/tilt quality is that of sadness. Singing the song through entirely in this quality will help to reinforce muscle memory and generally build stamina into the voice. It has the added benefit of being one of the safest qualities to use.

An angry/excited emotion emerges from high energy speech quality. There is no softness about this sound, neither in volume nor timbre. Adding twang resonance to this quality makes this high energy sound easier to produce, as well as reducing effort within the true vocal folds. Generally, any song will require a mixture of voice qualities, but for angry/excited emotions, speech quality predominates.

As the pitch rises up the scale, speech quality can be trained to turn into belt quality, with a corresponding increase in volume and physical effort. It is not wise to teach belt quality to young singers because of the stamina required to sustain it. ***(See The Essential Anatomy, Chapter 3 Making Sound – The Larynx, Voice Qualities; Training The Singing Voice, Chapter 1, Relating Sound to the Anatomy, Voice Qualities)***

This is a good moment to mention vibrato. Vibrato is a slight variation of pitch arising from the free vibration of the true vocal folds, accompanied by slight movement of the whole larynx due to the air flow. It makes the voice sound warmer and rounder. If there is too much vibrato, the voice may encompass a semitone, which then becomes a wobble, so it needs to be kept under control. Absence of vibrato creates the "white" voiced straight tone which is currently popular among exponents of Early Music. This sound comprises speech quality mixed with some thin-fold cry quality, and a predominance of head resonance.

Vibrato naturally occurs with thyroid tilt, when using sob/tilt or cry/tilt quality. Vibrato does not occur naturally in speech quality. It can be added to the tone for effect, particularly at the end of phrases. In this case, care must be taken to ensure that vibrato does not become extreme and turn into a wobble. ***(See Training The Singing Voice, Chapter 1, Relating Sound to The Anatomy, Vibrato)***

Building the Song into the Voice

Here are three choices of songs which are ideal for younger singers, and who may wish to build towards a graded singing exam, along with suggested methods of building them into the voice. This incorporates information from the preceding sections and shows how to use it practically in your teaching.

Folk song: My Father's Garden (Anon. French)

Classical Style
Art song: Cradle Song (Wiegenlied, Mozart, K.350)
Folk song: My Heart (Anon. Welsh)

My Father's Garden (Anon. French)

The first example appears in ABRSM Grade 1 Singing examination and may be found in the ABRSM Songbook 1. It is a traditional folk song, originally French ("Auprès de ma blonde") but with an English text here.

2
2. MY FATHER'S GARDEN
French traditional song, with words by Frederick Fowler
Simply
VOICE
PIANO
mp
1.&2. My fa - ther has a gar - den With
ma - ny li - lac trees, My fa - ther has a gar - den With
ma - ny li - lac trees, (1.)With branch-es spread -ing sky - wards And
(2.)With branch-es for the birds' nests And
sway - ing in the breeze.
flow - ers for the bees.
Come in-to our gar - den, come and see the
li - lacs there, Come in-to our gar - den, li - lacs ev - 'ry - where!
D.S.

Exercise:
Use the following steps to build the song.
1. Siren the tune ("ng").
2. Clap the rhythm.
3. Say the words of the song, clapping the rhythm as you do so.
4. Sing the tune using "na" on each note in place of the words.
5. Sing the tune again, using "wow" on each note in place of the words.
6. Sing the words.

Explanation of the above steps:

1. Sirening the tune initially frees the larynx, allowing it to move up and down in the throat, giving easy access to the range. ***(See Training The Singing Voice, Chapter 4, What is Good Singing? Sirening; Chapter 6, Suggested Warm-up Routine, Sirening)***
2. Clapping the rhythm develops physical awareness of the pulse in the song.
3.Speaking the words whilst clapping brings sound and rhythm together, therefore working both sides of the brain.
4.The "na" activates the resonators in the sinuses and the mouth, and gets the tongue moving
5.The "wow" uses the mouth as a resonator, preparing the student for the words of the song, as well as getting the jaw to move freely whilst widening the vocal tract.

In "My Father's Garden", the rhythm is vibrant and bouncy, which would indicate a happy mood; the words are cheerful and positive. The overall feeling is energetic and happy (a mixture of speech and cry/tilt qualities). The stated direction for performing this song is: "Simply".

Exercise :
To set up the larynx for these emotions, say "yeh" (as in "egg") in a happy and energetic way. The larynx will be raised and the thyroid cartilage tilted simply by doing this.

Then sing through the song, phrase by phrase using "yeh" instead of the words. The song will thus be sung in a mixture of speech and cry/tilt qualities.
Sing the song with the words, remembering the happy emotion.

The speech quality ensures that the words are clear. The cry/tilt quality enables the larynx to rise to the upper notes of the phrase with little effort.

Combining cry/tilt quality, with its thyroid tilt and higher larynx, and speech quality, achieves a blend of sound which is direct, clear and ideal for this song, turning the speech into singing. It is worth pointing out that sob/tilt quality, with a lowered larynx, should not be used in this song because this would produce a sad tone of voice. ***(See The Essential Anatomy, Chapter 3 Making Sound – The Larynx, Voice Qualities; Training The Singing Voice, Chapter 1, Relating Sound to the Anatomy, Voice Qualities)***

Cradle Song (Wiegenlied, Mozart, K.350)

Mozart's "Wiegenlied", is listed in the ABRSM singing Exam Grade 2 List B and may be found in the ABRSM Songbook 2.

When approaching such a song, it becomes clear that energy does not mean volume. This song is a lullaby and must be sung piano, with carefully shaped phrases. Piano singing does not mean that the sound is breathy. If there is no intensity in the performance, it will be dull and uninteresting, and will not communicate to an audience. ***(See Training The Singing Voice, Chapter 1, Relating Sound to the Anatomy, Volume)***

The predominant voice quality in this song should be sob/tilt quality, which will lower the larynx and soften the tone. This will happen naturally if your student has understood the text and style of the song. ***(See The Essential Anatomy, Chapter 3 Making Sound – The Larynx, Voice Qualities)***

There must be a heightened preparation in the body before you begin to sing, in order to support the tone. The breath support should be fully engaged even though the volume is not going to be great.

Exercise :

To acquire the necessary intensity :

1. Mime singing the first phrase of the song, whilst making sure that the necessary muscular activity is happening in the throat, mouth and body.
2. Begin to speak the phrases softly, with no breathiness.
3. Lower the larynx and engage the sob/tilt quality (think sad).
4. Sing the phrases with all of the above in place.

My Heart (Anon. Welsh)

The song "My Heart" (Anon. Welsh, with English words by John Thomas) may be found in the ABRSM Songbook 4. It is a folk song which should be approached in a classical style because of the way it has been adapted here.

The predominant voice quality in this song should be sob/tilt quality, which will lower the larynx and soften the tone. The song is all about sadness and woe, so the voice quality needs to reflect the emotional content. Cry/tilt would not be quite appropriate. ***(See The Essential Anatomy, Chapter 3 Making Sound – The Larynx, Voice Qualities; Training The Singing Voice, Chapter 1, Relating Sound to the Anatomy, Voice Qualities)***

Exercise:

To acquire the necessary intensity:

1. Siren ("ng") the song phrase by phrase, using a slide over the octave leap.
2. Reinforce the muscular activity of the octave leap by using the vowels "oo – ah – oo", with "oo" on the lower E, opening to the "ah" on the upper, and returning to the "oo" on the lower E. This will show how easily the upper note may be attained.
3. Lower the larynx and engage the sob/tilt quality (think sad) and repeat step 2.
4. Sing the song through, adding the words to the melody whilst maintaining the lowered larynx of sob/tilt.

Voice Qualities within Musical Theatre, Pop & Rock Music

When approaching more commercial repertoire, including the genres of musical theatre, pop and rock music, it is important to recognise which voice qualities to use which would differ from those we use within classical music.

In simple terms, the singer would generally not use sob/tilt quality within the musical theatre, pop and rock repertoire.

The two most common voice qualities which should be used are speech quality and cry/tilt, with the presence of twang resonance being added to a greater or lesser degree, dependant on how commercial the chosen song actually is.

Within the pre-1965 repertoire of musical theatre songs which have sustained legato line, and are commonly referred to as "legit" songs, the singer should use cry/tilt quality throughout, which will provide a required vibrato to the sound. Cry/tilt quality should also be used in any modern musical theatre song which has been written in the "legit" style up to, and including, the present day. If the singer uses sob/tilt quality instead of cry/tilt quality, then the overall tone will appear more classical, and therefore incorrect for this style of music.

For character songs, commercial songs within musical theatre, pop and rock songs, a great deal of speech quality should be used in sung phrases which are notated below the middle transition part of any voice. If a vibrato is required on the final note of such phrases, then the singer needs to use cry/tilt in order to create a nicely rounded finish to such phrases.

However, when any phrase is notated through and above the middle transition part of a voice within more commercial styles of musical theatre, pop and rock, then the singer needs to move the larynx into the cry/tilt position in order to facilitate safe transition into the upper part of the voice. This will always require an increase of effort within the supporting muscles of the breath support system.

It is within the repertoire of musical theatre, pop and rock that the singer has the option to use belt quality. The choice to use belt quality always has to be based on whether the note or notes in question are above the middle transition in any voice type and if it is emotionally appropriate to use this high energy, amplified quality at that point in the song. It is impossible to use belt quality below the middle transition in any voice type.
(See The Essential Anatomy, Chapter 3 Making Sound – The Larynx, Voice Qualities; Training The Singing Voice, Chapter 1, Relating Sound to the Anatomy, Voice Qualities)

Interpreting the Song

After the words and music have been learned, and the song is built into the voice, you can begin to explore ways of interpreting the song. This is a never-ending process related to a singer's developing musicianship, emotional maturity and communication skills.

The foundations of interpretation lie in:
recognising the genre of the song
recognising the style of the song

understanding the text
understanding the interplay of text and music
developing a personal response to the song

(See Appendix, Song Genres and Styles)

The singer should explore and develop their individual personal response to the song. This is what is known as "owning" the song. The degree of understanding and response on the part of the singer, will directly affect the quality of communication with the audience in performance.

Much of the interpretation falls into place as the song is being built into the voice. Good technical control allows the singer more freedom to interpret the song. The singer is then ready for the next step, which is performance.

SECTION SEVEN
Performance

What Makes for a Successful Performance?

Chapter One

Performance is the ultimate goal of all of the work undertaken in the teaching room. The performance may be to an audience, to an examiner or simply to the teacher. Whatever the circumstances, all performance requires the following:

connection with the audience
communication of the song
performance energy

The art of the performer lies not only in being able to communicate an idea or emotion to the audience, but to make that audience feel actively involved in the creative process. The audience should be moved to respond. The performer may not see the response, but when it happens, there is a change of energy in the performance space, and performer and audience alike feel uplifted.

Connection with the Audience

Connection with the audience begins at a physical but subliminal level. It has often been described as the performer's "presence". Research tells us that approximately 65% of a person's initial impact is dictated by their appearance. What they say and how they sound comes a poor second and third.

Subliminal signals are sent by such things as eye contact, posture, body language and what you are wearing. The audience will feel secure with a strong and comfortable presence, and will be more ready to engage with the performer.

After the initial connection is established, the emphasis changes to what you are saying and how you are saying it, in other words, communication and interpretation.

Communication of the Song

Communication of a song to an audience happens when the singer has good technical control, and has developed their own personal response to the content of the song. The singer's response has to include both music and words with equal measure.

A degree of research is always useful, especially when the song belongs to a character from an Opera or a Musical Theatre show. It helps the communication when the character's situation is understood by the singer.

The more the singer is involved with the song intellectually and emotionally, the greater his or her ownership of the song. They will then have more to share with the audience in performance.

An important part of communication is facial expression. The singer has to be an actor not only in the way the voice is used, but also in how it is physically expressed. A good technique means that there will be no residual tension in the neck, jaw and mouth, which leaves the face free to express the emotion contained in the song.

Performance Energy

The other key to connecting with the audience can be termed "performance energy". We use energy to walk across a room. We use a different form of energy to engage in a sporting activity. One energy is greater than the other. Performing demands a special form of heightened energy.

Performance energy brings about a state of mental alertness and physical readiness which lifts the singing of a song out of the ordinary into something special. It is life being lived intensely and communicated to an audience.

This heightened energy requires intense concentration from the performer, so that, even if he or she seems to be doing nothing, the audience feels that energy and intensity. They become part of the performance in a two-way communication, where the energy of the audience combines with that of the performer.

The performer's heightened energy must be controlled. If it is released all at once, the result can be disappointing. Stillness and soft singing can often be much more powerful than big gestures and loud singing. But they all equally need intensity and focussed energy. Such control will only come about through building the song into the voice step by step.

Preparing for Performance

Chapter Two

Thorough musical preparation and rehearsal are the first steps in preparing for a successful performance. You should also give thought to the way you wish to present yourself to the audience in your physical appearance.

Rehearsing

The French word for rehearsal is "répétition". Successful performance is the outcome of creative repetition. Each time the phrase, section or entire song is repeated in rehearsal, the music should be brought more and more to life and closer to performance.

The singer rarely performs alone. Sometimes, they may sing an unaccompanied song, such as a folk song. Or they may accompany themselves on an instrument, such as the guitar or piano. Even on these occasions, the rehearsal process is the next step on from the musical preparation. Throughout this process, it is important to be thinking of the three main points mentioned above –connection, communication, and energy.

Memorising

The convention of Oratorio allows the singer to have the music before them in performance. Other forms, such as Song Recital, Opera and Musical Theatre performances, demand that the singer memorise the work.

Committing music and words to memory gives the singer increased ownership of the music, and opens up a greater freedom of communication with the audience. Some singers find memorisation an easy process, others do not. However, it is worth persevering to achieve this ideal, and it becomes easier with practice.

The foundation for committing songs to memory is repetition. This repetitive process should not be sterile and mindless, but creative and enjoyable. It happens during the period of musical preparation, building the song into the voice and rehearsal for performance.

Learning music and learning words take place in different parts of the brain. It becomes easier to memorise if you address one of these at a time. Most singers find it easier to commit the music to memory rather than the words. In this case, it is worthwhile to treat the lyrics as text which can be recited independently of the music. After the words have been committed to memory in this way, the process of rehearsal reconnects them with the music.

Getting Ready for your Audience

Personal appearance is the next step in preparing for performance, particularly in Recital, Concert and Oratorio singing. If the singer feels happy with the way they look, their personal confidence will be enhanced and evident to the audience.

Care should be taken in making sure that the concert clothing is in good repair and flattering. Ladies should consider co-ordinating their choice of gown with other performers, so that clashes of colour or style do not occur.

When the occasion is less formal, it is safer to be conservative in choice of clothes, unless the presentation is a semi-staged version of a Musical Theatre show or an Opera, when an attempt at characterisation through dress would be appropriate.

Taking pride in your personal appearance for a performance has a positive influence on performer and audience alike.

Performance Nerves

Performance brings the fruit of learning and practice before an audience. It is an intensive experience which demands high levels of concentration, energy and sheer nerve. It carries with it elements of stress and fear which can either undermine the performance, or lift it to a new level. The question is, how do you consistently achieve the latter result rather than the former?

The singer can go a long way to make the performance more of a celebration than an ordeal. To begin with, you must face up to the fact that performance is a stressful experience, and understand what happens to the singing voice when under stress.

Strong emotions, such as nervousness and fear, generate a lot of energy, which comes from an increased flow of adrenalin. This energy can cause the vocal mechanism to shut down. The vocal folds tend to close so that breath flow is restricted, and the false vocal folds tend to clamp over them to reinforce this closure. This is called "constriction" ***(See the sections "The Essential Anatomy" and "Training the Singing Voice").***

When constriction occurs, even though the true vocal folds manage to open for breathing, the false vocal folds may not be fully retracted, which interferes with any attempt to sing. Constriction impairs vocal range, volume and quality. The breathing changes, so that long phrases seem impossible and short gasps are all that can be managed.

The solution is to change the energy from a "closing-down" form to an "opening-up" one, thus changing it into "performance energy". To achieve this, the false vocal folds need to be kept fully retracted and the walls of the pharynx should be anchored (see exercises in section on "Training the Singing Voice"). The breath support system should be fully engaged, and correct posture maintained throughout.

In this way, nerves are changed into an energy which sustains the singer and the song, and the work achieved in the teaching room will be brought alive in performance.

Singing with a Microphone

On some occasions, the singer may have to work with a microphone. This may happen in two ways. Firstly, there may be a small microphone taped to the head, as in Musical Theatre shows or in some large scale Opera productions. Secondly, there may be a standing or hand-held microphone, such as for cabaret, or rock and pop performances.

In both cases, the singer is dependent upon the quality of the microphone and sound system. The overall balance is controlled by the sound engineer at the mixing desk. With head microphones, the singer has no control and should sing as if the microphone were not there.

With standing and hand-held microphones, the singer can achieve some control by the way they hold the microphone and the distance from the mouth. Microphones have differing response levels, so it is advisable for the singer to rehearse with the microphone prior to performance.

Performing with Others

Chapter Three

Singing with an Accompanist

The singer is never truly a soloist, unless singing unaccompanied. For the most part, a singer will be working with another musician, usually a pianist. It is helpful to view this as a duet, an equal partnership working together to make music. The partnership is established by both performers listening to each other.

Most song repertoire begins with an introduction on the accompanying instrument, even if this is just a chord. The song starts from the first note, not from where the voice enters, so the singer must participate in the creation of mood from the outset.

Similarly, the song does not end when the singer stops singing, but after the last note has died away. In many cases, as with Schumann, there may be a long postlude to the song. The singer should hold the mood throughout.

Wherever possible, rehearsal time should be arranged in advance of the performance, competition, examination or audition. Practising together strengthens the partnership, which makes for a better performance.

Apart from a few conventions, such as Oratorio, the singer will be expected to perform from memory, whilst the accompanist usually plays from a copy of the music.

The singer has several responsibilities of a practical nature if the partnership with the accompanist is to work well. The copy of the music should be presented to the accompanist in a form in which it is readily playable. If it is tattered, unreadable and falls off the piano, the accompanist will be unreasonably distracted and the performance will suffer.

The singer should also ensure that the accompanist has a copy of the music in the key in which it is to be performed. Transposition at sight is a rare skill, and the singer should not ordinarily expect the accompanist to possess this skill.

Singing with Another Singer

When working with another singer, the quality of the listening becomes even more important. Achieving a true blend of voices is a process which begins in rehearsal and is fulfilled in performance. Listening to the other voice, rather than your own, will help to establish the balance in volume and tone.

Important considerations when working with another singer are:

shaping of phrases
choosing where to breathe
dynamics
accuracy of pitch
blend of tone

In shaping phrases, the singers should complement each other, not act in opposition.

Similarly with breathing, both singers must agree where to breathe.

The harmony dictates which voice predominates at any given time, and so the dynamic must be adjusted to take this into account. There are also occasions when the voices must be equally matched in volume, for example when singing the same phrase in thirds.

Singing in tune is even more important when there is another voice working in harmony. Listening carefully to the other voice is so important here.

Blend of tone (timbre) can vary according to the type of song. The singers should be able to match each other in terms of voice quality where required, or to create a contrast. For example, the Flower Duet from "Lakmé" by Delibes requires two female voices, often singing in close harmony, to blend equally. However, the two characters singing the duet "You're Just in Love" from "Call Me Madame" by Irving Berlin, have separate tunes which are of contrasting mood, which require different voice qualities and which are sung together.

Singing in Ensembles

When working in a group, such as a choir, a singer may not be able to hear their own voice. This may be disorientating, especially for the inexperienced singer. The temptation may be to sing louder in order to hear themselves above the others. The voice may become pushed and tired because of this.

In such cases, the singer should trust the sensation of singing and feel the voice working properly, rather than trying to hear themselves above the others, which will only lead to forcing the sound. The singer should understand that the art of ensemble singing resides in the blending of voices. If each voice were to compete, the ensemble suffers.

Some choral conductors are keen to warm up the voices at the start of the choir rehearsal. However, the singer should not solely depend upon the conductor for exercises to warm up the voice. They should arrive at rehearsal or performance having undertaken their own system of warm-up appropriate to their voice. This should normally have been worked out with their singing teacher. ***(See Training The Singing Voice, Chapter 6, Suggested Warm-up Routine)***

Healthy Practices

Chapter Four

Building Stamina

Performances can vary in their demands on the singer. Standing up and delivering a folk song is less energetic than singing an operatic role. The singer should build the strength to sustain whatever demands the performance may require during the rehearsal period.

Daily practice routines are vital in maintaining the stamina levels sufficient to meet the demands of the performance. There are also exercises to build stamina described in the section "Training the Singing Voice". ***(See Training The Singing Voice, Chapter 5, Practice; Chapter 6, Suggested Warm-up Routine; Chapter 7, Further Training Exercises)***

The Importance of Rest

Stamina develops by having a period of rest after an intensive workout. Muscles are used vigorously in a training or practice session, but the actual strength is built up in the recovery period afterwards. Constantly working muscles without allowing them to rest weakens them, rather than strengthens them.

When working towards a performance it is necessary to take this into account, especially on the day itself. Warming up too vigorously, or constantly practising that worrying high note will not necessarily help the performance. When engaged in a series of night-after-night performances, the performer should go to bed instead of a party, and rest during the day prior to each performance.

Warming Down

Muscles should be warmed up before intensive use. Similarly, they should be warmed down after intensive use. This helps them to return to their normal length and condition. Gentle exercises such as the siren help the muscles used in singing to recover. The siren is described in the section "Training the Singing Voice". ***(See Training The Singing Voice, Chapter 6, Suggested Warm-up Routine, Sirening)***

Health Issues

The singing voice is so easily affected by atmospheric changes, temperature, diet, poor health and a number of other factors. Proper training helps the singer to overcome the adverse effects of many of these, and to be able to perform well when conditions are not ideal.

However, it is best to avoid situations which may put the voice under strain. The most obvious of these is to avoid such places as smokey rooms, loud environments where you have to strain to be heard, or where allergic responses may occur. It is also worth mentioning that some singers may have an allergic response to perfume, so be considerate of other singers with your use of this.

The larynx can be affected by acid reflux brought about by eating spicy food and too close to bed time. Leave a good two hours after eating before you retire at night. ***(See Troubleshooting, Chapter 1, Health Issues, Acid Reflux)***

Alcohol dehydrates the vocal folds and impairs the way they function. It is best to avoid drinking alcohol before a performance, and in moderation at other times. ***(See Troubleshooting, Chapter 1, Health Issues, Dehydration; Alcohol)***

The danger of smoking cigarettes is well known. The damage to the vocal folds caused by smoking can seriously affect the singer's performance. Recreational drugs can have the same effect. ***(See Troubleshooting, Chapter 1, Health Issues, Smoking; Recreational Drugs)***

Some medicines prescribed by doctors have a dehydrating effect upon the vocal folds, which can make it difficult for the singer to produce the tone and which affect the range by taking away the high notes. Where this is the case, further consultation with the doctor should be encouraged. ***(See Troubleshooting, Chapter 1, Health Issues, Dehydration)***

Finally, singers often become stressed about colds and sore throats, and wonder whether or not they should sing. As a general rule, it is inadvisable to sing if there is an infection in the laryngo-pharynx where the vocal folds are inflamed. Damage can be caused if the vocal folds are used strenuously when suffering from a viral infection. ***(See Troubleshooting, Chapter 1, Health Issues, Colds; Persistent Sore Throats)***

A sore throat in the oro-pharynx usually means that the infection has not reached the larynx, and so it may be safe to sing. If it becomes difficult to sing because of excessive catarrh and inflammation of the throat, then it is best to be guided by your symptoms and rest. ***(See Troubleshooting, Chapter 1, Health Issues, Colds; Persistent Sore Throats; Catarrh)***

Sirening is an excellent way of checking the condition of the vocal folds. If the siren doesn't work without force, something is not right. ***(See Training The Singing Voice, Chapter 6, Suggested Warm-up Routine, Sirening)***

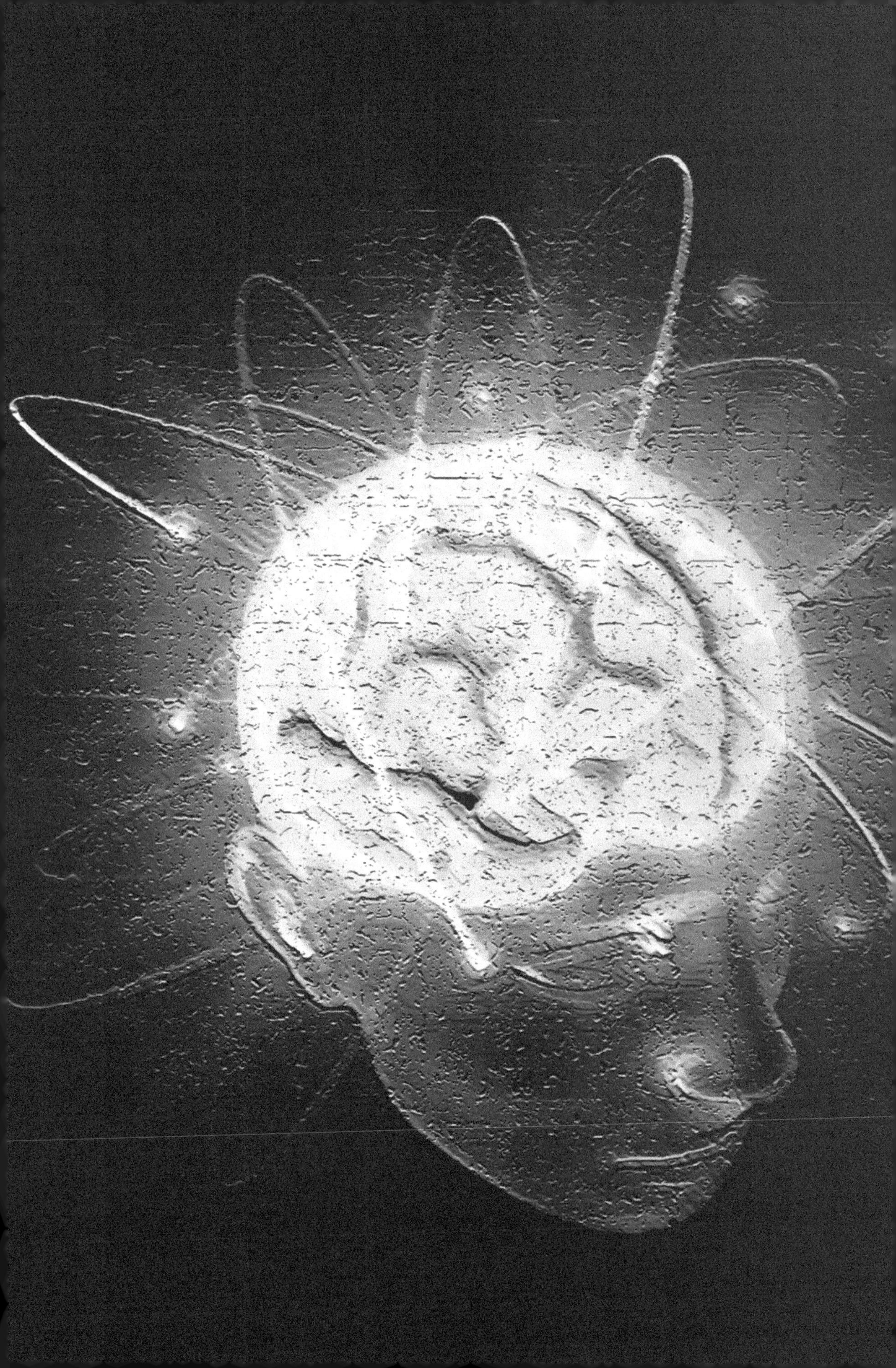

SECTION EIGHT
The Psychology of Singing

The Psychology of Singing

Singing is a fundamental impulse. Babies sing in their prams before they can speak. Singing is good for us. It is a form of cardiovascular exercise which also stimulates the pineal gland to release feel-good hormones.

There is a great physical satisfaction to be found in the act of singing, and when combined with its creative, intellectual, emotional and musical components, it becomes a powerful vehicle for expression.

Previous chapters have looked at the physical and creative components of singing, and now it is important to explore the psychological aspects.

Self-Perception

How many times have you heard an adult say: "I can't sing, I'm tone deaf!" How has this come about, when true tone-deafness is extremely rare? This mental attitude has probably arisen because, at some stage in a person's childhood, someone has made an adverse comment about their voice. Such negative comments can result in a child shutting down both ears and voice, believing they cannot sing. This may prevent the development of aural skills and limit the development of the muscular system of the voice.

Anything which stifles the natural impulse to sing must be wrong. Anybody who tells a child that he or she cannot sing is doing an injustice to that child. Being told that they have an unpleasant voice, or that they cannot sing, does immense damage to the child's perception of itself and its abilities.

Most children can sing if they are encouraged to. The adult who claims not to be able to sing was probably deprived of this encouragement as a child.

Confidence

Adverse criticism of this kind is destructive. It is more constructive to build a child's confidence. Confidence is a key issue in releasing the singing voice, and must always be allowed to develop. You should create an environment where your students, especially the shy ones, feel sufficiently at ease to explore their voice. Freedom to explore in an uninhibited way leads to the development of range, dynamics and vocal colour.

Inhibition gets in the way of the development of the voice and can suppress freedom and energy. The natural tendency of the larynx is to close down. Inhibition, nervousness, lack of confidence, and emotional upset all contribute to bringing about such a closure. Singing becomes very difficult, if not impossible, under these circumstances. Inhibition can stifle the personal development of the singer.

Mental Approach

A student's mental approach influences their development. If their attitude is not right, the physical and creative processes necessary for good singing will be hindered. For example, where the student has a preconception that they already know how to sing, they may be unwilling to change established habits of voice production in order to learn new and better ones. This prejudice is often hard to break down, and blocks the way to progress.

Creating new and better habits of vocal production takes a singer out of their comfort zone. Nobody feels safe exploring new territory, especially if they felt secure in the old ways. New methods should be balanced by encouragement and positive reinforcement so that the mental attitude does not turn to one of resistance.

Motivation

A singer's development depends very much on positive mental attitudes, such as motivation. However, motivation can be reinforced either positively or negatively. It is useful for the teacher to consider the reasons why a student may or may not be progressing as expected, in order to remove those obstacles where possible.

Positive Motivational Forces

parental encouragement and praise – a student will progress faster when parents express personal interest in their achievements
rewarding practice – practising can be an isolated activity and requires self-discipline; praise and a system of awards will encourage the student to persist
successful performance will always motivate the student to continue – the opportunity to show an audience what you can do is a reward in itself
positive analysis of poor performance – student know when they have not done their best; discuss where they went wrong and show them how to improve

a system of measured achievement – feedback on progress from exams, concerts, performance, competitions and festivals is a vital stimulant
revisiting previously-learnt repertoire – singing a song which once presented technical difficulty, but no longer does, shows the student that they have made progress
achievable goals – realistic goals should be tailored to the ability of the individual student; even a little success is a big encouragement
social involvement – working with others in environments such as local choirs, music festivals and amateur operatic groups stimulates development within a recreational context
stress-releasing activity – singing is a healthy pursuit and can be therapeutic
Student involvement in repertoire choices – a sense of participation in the whole process keeps the student's interest
growing self-confidence – the more capable a student feels, the more motivated they become
variety – freshness in lesson content, approach to repertoire, and teaching style will keep a student stimulated and motivated

Negative Motivational Forces

social pressures – appearing to be different from members of one's own age group is a serious disincentive; choice of friends and company is very important
parental disinterest – lack of encouragement and interest from a parent may suggest that a child's achievements are of little value
practice issues – practice is necessary for progress, but must not be perceived just as a chore, or even a punishment
forced pace of learning – expectations beyond the student's ability are disheartening
impossible goals – unrealistic challenges demoralise the student by inviting failure
unresolved technical problems – persistent technical problems must be addressed for progress to be observable
dislike of repertoire being offered by teacher – the repertoire must be meaningful to the student, or become so with study, or they will lose interest
bad performance – consistently low standards in performance are demoralising; better not to perform until an acceptable standard has been attained in the lesson
lack of fun in lessons – students learn better when the lesson is enjoyable; children learn through play

Personal Fulfilment

You should always have, as your foremost consideration, the overall personal development of your student. Teaching should not concentrate solely on examination qualifications, entrance to music college or the ultimate goal of a professional career.
If a singer judges their success only by the yardstick of a qualification, music becomes a commodity to be used and put aside when no longer needed. It should be an integral part of their spiritual and emotional lives.

It is just as valid to pursue singing for personal pleasure as it is to aspire to professional standards. Some singers may never reach the level of technical expertise necessary to become a professional singer. However, this should not be a reason for discouraging anyone! Singing is healthy, both physically and psychologically, and can lead to a sense of personal fulfilment.

SECTION NINE
Further Development

Further Development

Choirs and Societies

Any singer, whatever their level of attainment, should consider opportunities afforded by local choirs, music societies and amateur operatic groups. Apart from the social aspects, these organisations give singers a chance to use their talents and their training on a regular basis.

Sometimes the repertoire can be quite adventurous, and the learning curve of a performance can excite enthusiasm for continuing study and development. Usually membership entails attending an audition.

Normally rehearsals involve teaching you the music, but you will be expected to do some learning in your own time. Most rehearsals will commence with a vocal warm-up, but it advisable for you to have done your own vocal warm-up before you attend each rehearsal, so that your voice is ready to work.

When working in a group, you may not be able to hear your own voice. This may be disorientating, especially if you are not used to singing in a group situation. The temptation may be to sing louder in order to hear your own voice above the others. Be careful! Your voice may become pushed and tired if you do. If you come away from a rehearsal with a sore throat or vocal fatigue, you are not singing correctly.

You should learn to trust the sensation of your voice working properly, rather than try to hear yourself above the others.

Preparation for Auditions

Auditions are a fact of life for those considering entry to colleges, universities, choirs, music societies and operatic groups, and are a constant feature in the world of the professional singer. They can be nerve-wracking experiences, when all technique can appear to fly out of the window! It is essential that you be thoroughly prepared for these events. The choice of repertoire is vital; choose music which will show you off to best advantage.

Repertoire which pushes you to the limits of your technical ability should best be avoided in these circumstances. You should select music which has been built into your voice and is comfortable for your range and is not too dramatic for your voice. You will give a better performance in audition if you sing repertoire which suits you, and which has been well-rehearsed beforehand. Never take untoward risks at auditions! Always show what you can do now, rather than what you would like to do one day.

Which College Or Conservatoire?

If a singer wishes to take their training to a further stage, it becomes important to explore where to go next. There is a wide range of courses available beyond Grade 8 and "A" Level, including classical, musical theatre, rock, pop and jazz courses.

In order to make the most suitable choice of course and institution, your level of ability and range of interests must be weighed against what is on offer. Universities offer a more theoretical approach to study. If you wish to undertake practical performance training, you might consider other options.

Classical singers would need to look at the range of classically-based music colleges, and explore the range of courses which they offer to see whether they match your criteria of ability and interests. Specialist opera courses should not be encouraged for young singers at undergraduate level. They are more of a post-graduate level of study and for voices which are more mature.

There are a host of courses on offer if you are interested in musical theatre. These are usually at drama colleges rather than at traditional conservatoires, and are of a vocational nature for those who wish to work in the profession.

There are an increasing number of courses for rock, pop and jazz study on offer at both university and vocationally-orientated colleges. Both student and teacher should consult professional careers guidance available on-line and from schools, colleges and local government.

Curriculum Vitae (CV)

At certain times in your career, you will be asked to provide a resumé (curriculum vitae) of your training and experience. This is a standard requirement for applications for entrance to colleges and universities, as well as some auditions.

In the music profession, it is expected that the CV will be up-to-date, and include contact details, qualifications, prizes and awards, voice type, a list of your singing teachers past and present, performing experience and future engagements.

It is good practice to set out a personal CV under these headings, and to make new entries as they occur.

SECTION TEN
Troubleshooting

CHAPTER ONE
Health Issues

CHAPTER TWO
Recognising and Remedying Vocal Difficulties

Health Issues

Chapter One

The singing voice can be affected by many different factors. It is natural for the teacher to look to technical issues to resolve problems, but sometimes the root causes lie outside of the teaching studio. Factors such as changes of atmosphere, temperature, diet and poor health affect the voice. It is important to consider these, and other health issues, when trying to resolve vocal problems which do not appear to respond to training.

Vocal difficulties may sometimes be caused by health concerns, or even physical damage, over which the student and teacher may seem to have little control. Here are a few suggestions which could help to alleviate some of these concerns.

Colds

Singers often become stressed about colds and sore throats, and wonder whether or not they should sing. As a general rule, it is inadvisable to sing if there is an infection in the laryngo-pharynx ***(See The Essential Anatomy, Chapter 4, The Throat [Pharynx])*** where the vocal folds are inflamed. Damage can be caused if the vocal folds are used strenuously when suffering from a viral infection.

Often, however, the cold may be confined to the nose, sinuses and oro-pharynx. In such cases, where the vocal folds are not affected, it may be safe to sing for short periods. Resonance may be affected by the thickening of the mucosal lining of the throat and vocal folds, due to infection. Whilst there is no known cure for a cold, symptoms can be eased by gargling with warm salty water.

Persistent Sore Throats

It is important to ascertain whether recurrent sore throats are caused by misuse of the voice or by infection and allergy. If the voice is continually tired, the teacher should consider whether the cause of this may be bad posture, especially collapse of the spine at the back of the neck, lack of anchoring in the pharynx (***See The Essential Anatomy, Chapter 1, Posture)***, lack of effective breath support or forced air pressure (***See The Essential Anatomy, Chapter 2, Breathing – Breath Support)***. Strain in the throat may result from these conditions.

Aching of the muscles in the neck is not necessarily a symptom of strain. It may be that the muscles have been properly worked and are in the process of being strengthened. If, however, the aching is continual, then strain must be suspected and these postural issues addressed.

A sore throat may also mean that there is an infection of the pharynx. If it becomes difficult to sing because of excessive catarrh and inflammation of the throat, then it is best to be guided by your symptoms and rest. Inhaling steam is a good way of clearing sinuses and helping the pharynx recover from infection.

Hoarseness

The voice may sound hoarse because of a problem at the level of the vocal folds. This may be caused by persistent constriction ***(See The Essential Anatomy, Chapter 3, Making The Sound – The Larynx)***, or by a temporary condition, such as an infection or vocal fatigue. If there is an infection, the vocal folds themselves are inflamed in some way, and should be allowed to recover before further use. Similarly with vocal fatigue, the muscles closing the vocal folds need to rest in order to recover their strength.

Persistent hoarseness and tiredness in the throat may indicate a more deep-seated problem, and should be referred to a medical practitioner.

Catarrh

The vocal folds, the pharynx and the sinuses are covered by a layer of mucous. The quality of the mucous affects the functioning of the vocal folds. Catarrh is a thickening of the mucous and may be caused by a virus or an allergy. If catarrh persists for longer than several weeks, the root cause of the problem should be investigated further.

Allergies

Allergies are common in today's society, and can play havoc with the voice. They may be seasonal, such as hay fever, or chronic, such as allergy to house mites. There are also allergies sparked by contact with such things as soaps, perfumes and household cleaners. They are often treated by antihistamine medication.

Medication which alleviates the symptoms also may interfere with the proper functioning of the voice. This is usually caused by the dehydrating effects of the medicines. Sometimes they may cause muscle weakness. It is important to work out with your doctor which medication is appropriate for you as a singer.

Asthma

Asthma is a chronic disease of the respiratory system. The airways can constrict, become inflamed, and produce excessive amounts of mucous. This may be triggered off by allergy, exercise, emotional stress or even contact with cold air. Symptoms such as wheezing, shortness of breath and coughing may be in evidence. Most people suffering from asthma are on medication. Singing greatly helps those who suffer from asthma to cope with their symptoms by strengthening the breath support system. When the symptoms of asthma occur, they will interfere with the ability to sing. They can be alleviated with medication, but care should also be taken to counteract the dehydrating effects of these drugs.

Acid Reflux

The larynx may be irritated by drinking alcohol and eating food, especially spicy food, too close to bed time. Acid reflux occurs when partially digested food rises back up into the oesophagus, even as far as the oro-pharynx.

This causes inflammation of the vocal tract, and stops the voice from working at its best. All in all, common sense and moderation should prevail. Leave a good two hours after eating before you retire at night. Where the situation is chronic, consult a medical practitioner.

Damage Through Trauma

Damage may have been caused to the larynx through trauma or previous misuse. For example, nodules caused by bad vocal habits can be treated medically and with speech and language therapy. The results are generally excellent.

However, although good training may resolve some problems, a cure may not be truly possible in all cases, especially where long term damage has occurred. In these cases, both singer and teacher must realise that full potential may never be reached, but a degree of enjoyment can still be derived from learning to sing.

Strain

There are many situations which may put the voice under strain. The most obvious of these are such places as smoky rooms, loud environments where you have to strain to be heard, or where allergic responses may occur. Strain may also come from singing too loudly and with insufficient breath support. Vocal strain may show in an inability to sing softly or to siren through the entire range. Even if there are no other symptoms, such as a sore throat, the singer should ascertain how the strain was caused and avoid those situations in future.

Dehydration

Dehydration can be caused by atmospheric conditions such as hot, dry weather, central heating and air conditioning. It can also be caused by some medications, alcohol, smoking and use of recreational drugs. It is such a common condition, yet it is so easily overlooked.
The quality of the mucosal lining of the vocal folds and throat is important to the proper functioning of the voice. If the mucous is dry or thick, then the voice will be adversely affected. The solution is to drink small amounts of water regularly, in order to keep dehydration at bay. Singers should ensure that they have a good, regular intake of water to maintain a healthy condition of the vocal tract.

Medication

Some medicines prescribed by doctors have a dehydrating effect upon the delicate tissues of the vocal folds, which can make it difficult for the singer to produce the tone. They can also affect the singer's range by taking away the high notes. Where this is the case, further consultation with the doctor should be encouraged.

Tea and Coffee

The caffeine in tea and coffee not only dehydrates the body but also affects the central nervous system. Large consumption of these beverages should be avoided.

Carbonated Drinks

Soft drinks which contain caffeine dehydrate the body. Further irritation to the vocal folds is caused by other carbonated drinks, as they increase the acidity of the stomach and regurgitate into the throat when you burp. They can also cause acid reflux.

Alcohol

Alcohol dehydrates the vocal folds and impairs the way they function. It is best to avoid drinking alcohol before a performance, and in moderation at other times.

Smoking

The danger of smoking cigarettes is well known. The damage to the vocal folds caused by smoking can seriously affect the singing voice. The breath support system is undermined because of the damage to the lungs. It is an unfortunate habit which should be strenuously discouraged.

Recreational Drugs

Most recreational drugs cause damage because of the way they are inhaled over the vocal folds and the dehydrating effects once they are in the system. They also have a negative effect on the central nervous system and can cause serious complications for health at all levels. Avoid them.

Recognising and Remedying Vocal Difficulties

Chapter Two

Every sound we make is the result of muscular activity. Muscular action controls the breath support system, allows the movement of the component parts of the larynx, engages the resonators and changes the shape of the mouth and pharynx.

If the muscles are working properly, the voice will emerge as desired. If there is an imbalance or imperfect action of the muscles, the voice will be adversely affected. When you hear a sound, you should be able to analyse how that sound is being produced. If the sound is incorrectly produced, your analysis will go a long way in helping you to remedy it.

Here are the main issues which you will meet on a regular basis. You will have already read about them in the sections ***"The Essential Anatomy"*** and ***"Training the Singing Voice"***, where you will also find exercises to remedy them.

Collapsed posture
Tuning problems
Bleat
Wobble
Register changes ("breaks" in the voice)
Fear of high notes
Forcing high notes
Cracking on high notes
Gaining volume through force
Inability to support long phrases/Short breath
Breathy sound
Constriction
Nasality
Tension in the jaw
Tension in the root of the tongue
Wrong positioning of the tongue

Collapsed Posture

Collapsed posture is a misalignment of the spine commonly called slouching. When present, it means that the breath support system and the anchoring systems for the larynx cannot work properly. The diaphragm cannot work effectively because there is little room for it to move if the upper part of the body is collapsed. Standing up straight gives it space to move freely.

The larynx cannot work properly if the back of the neck is collapsed and the jaw is protruding. Singers should be helped to understand that the alignment of the spine is a crucial issue, and must be alert and ready to correct bad posture. ***(See The Essential Anatomy, Chapter 1, Posture)***

Tuning Problems

Real tone deafness is a very rare condition. Singing in tune is a function of correct breath support and position of the larynx in the throat. If your student can recognise a pitch, you can train them to reproduce that pitch in the voice. If your student has difficulty recognising differences in pitch, then aural training to correct this should be the first step.

To correct poor tuning, make sure that the larynx is moving freely in the throat and that the breath support system is energised. ***(See Training the Singing Voice, Chapter 1, Relating Sound to the Anatomy, Pitch)***

Bleat

This fast, unpleasant vibrato arises from incorrect air flow. The true vocal folds vibrate when air flows over them and they move together. This is called adduction.

The vocal folds also act as a valve to control the flow of air. When the true vocal folds try to control the air flow at the same time as they are vibrating to speak or sing, the voice is affected and sounds squeezed. The resulting sound is a bleat. The air flow in singing should be controlled by the breath support system, not by the larynx. ***(See Training the Singing Voice, Chapter 1, Relating Sound to the Anatomy, Vibrato)***

Wobble

A wobble in the voice is really a wide vibrato, caused by loss of breath support or too much air pressure. It may be remedied by correcting these and adding firmer neck anchoring. ***(See Training The Singing Voice, Chapter 1, Relating Sound to the Anatomy, Vibrato)***

Register Changes ("breaks" in the voice)

As pitch rises and falls, the larynx also rises and falls in the throat. The true vocal folds also change in length and thickness or thinness. Sometimes these changes can be quite abrupt, which sound as if the voice is changing gear.

Teachers and singers have even referred to having different "voices" (head or chest) on either side of these gear changes. In truth, there is only one voice. The singer must learn to control the gear changes by controlling the relative thickness of the vocal folds and the position of the larynx in the throat. Sirening is a great help here.

The notion of a "head" or "chest" voice arises from the resonance being felt in these areas. Singers need to mix these resonances and sensations so that the tone quality is balanced throughout the range. This will also help to smooth out any gear changes, so that the transition from one register to another becomes smooth. ***(See Training the Singing Voice, Chapter 4, What Is good Singing? There is a wide range of pitch without strain)***

Fear of High Notes

Pitch is determined by a combination of the position of the larynx in the throat and the air pressure powered by the breath support system.

High notes will be attained more easily when the larynx is relatively high in the throat, the vocal fold mass is relatively thin and when both of these are underpinned by proper energy from the breath support system. Gentle sirening helps the larynx move more freely in the throat.

A useful way to access high notes is to get the larynx into a high position by sirening upwards, then to increase energy from the breath support system. Open the siren into a vowel such as "ee" or "ah". This gentle approach should help eliminate any fear. It is important that "high" is not associated with "loud" in the singer's mind. ***(See Training the Singing Voice, Chapter 6, Suggested Warm-up Routines, Sirening)***

Forcing High Notes

Pitch is determined by a combination of the position of the larynx in the throat and the air pressure powered by the breath support system.

If the larynx is too low in the throat and the vocal folds are too thick, the only way to achieve a higher pitch is by increasing air pressure and driving the air. The sound becomes a scream as air is forced through the vocal folds. The larynx is placed under too much strain and tires quickly. Persistent forcing in this way can lead to long term damage.
High notes should be approached initially with thinner folds and a higher larynx. When they can be produced this way, greater weight may then be added to the voice by increasing air pressure and thickening the folds. ***(See Training the Singing Voice, Chapter 1, Relating Sound to the Anatomy, Volume)***

Cracking on High Notes

Cracking on high notes usually occurs because there is too much air pressure beneath the vocal folds, the larynx is not sufficiently high in the throat and the anchoring is weak. Too much air pressure means that the breath support system is not sufficiently energised.

There is also a psychological aspect. The singer may be worried about the note, which can lead to constriction in the throat as well as a lack of preparation in the body. Sometimes, having attained the note, the confidence fails and the support and anchoring give way. Thorough preparation in the body in advance of the note, mental preparation, and realising that "high" does not mean "loud", will help to resolve this problem. ***(See Training the Singing Voice, Chapter 1, Relating Sound to the Anatomy, Volume)***

Gaining Volume Through Force

The volume of a voice is produced by the combination of air pressure and relative thickness of the true vocal folds. When the singer starts to drive air across the true vocal folds in order to be louder, there is a danger of traumatising the larynx. The strength of muscles within the throat has to be built up steadily over a long period of time in order to withstand sustained high breath pressure. They will become weak when constantly forced to overwork.

The carrying power of the voice depends on the correct balance of air pressure and use of resonators. Adding twang resonance is an excellent way to make the voice project. Loudness and carrying power are different issues. ***(See Training the Singing Voice, Chapter 1, Relating Sound to the Anatomy, Volume)***

Inability to Support Long Phrases/Short Breath

There are several causes for this, chief among which is releasing too much air when singing. If the breath support system is not working with enough energy and the vocal folds are not closing properly, then air is wasted and the longer phrases will be difficult to sustain.

There may be a medical condition, such as asthma or a heart condition, which means that oxygen uptake is not efficient. The singer will want to breath more frequently in such cases.

The "Three Blind Mice" exercise in "Training the Singing Voice" is excellent for developing the ability to sustain a longer phrase, even for those singers with medical conditions. In any case, when the singer needs to breathe, there will always be a way to achieve this whilst maintaining the line of the song. ***(See Training the Singing Voice, Chapter 7, Further Training Exercises, Sustained Breathing – Three Blind Mice)***

Breathy Sound

Breathy sound arises because too much air is escaping, usually because the vocal folds are not coming together properly. Girls at puberty may go through a phase where the voice is breathy. This is because the cartilage systems of the larynx grow at a faster rate than the muscles which move them. The situation resolves itself over time. ***(See The Developing Voice, Chapter 1, Girls' Voices)***

Exercises in adduction of the vocal folds help to overcome the problem. Using gentle glottal onsets, on a variety of vowels and pitches in the middle range of the voice, are a very good way of strengthening the muscles which adduct the true vocal folds.

Persistent breathiness may indicate a problem at vocal fold level and should be referred to a medical practitioner.

Constriction

The easiest way to describe the sound of constriction is that the voice sounds squeezed and unpleasantly rough. The air is not flowing easily across the vocal folds. This rasping sound indicates that the true vocal folds are not functioning properly. The false vocal folds are interfering with the action of the true folds.

A singer needs to ensure that the air flow is being properly controlled by the breath support system and not by tension at the larynx. Any tension within the larynx will usually be caused by the action of the false vocal folds. These may be retracted by silent laughing.

The unconstricted voice sounds clear, not squeezed and raspy. Constriction is very unhealthy for the true vocal folds and can lead to long-term problems. ***(See The Essential Anatomy, Chapter 3, Making The Sound – The Larynx)***

Nasality

Nasality is the sound produced when the voice resonates predominantly in the nose. It is not always desirable, as it muffles the tone.

Constant nasality arises from the inappropriate use of nasal resonators. In such cases the muscles of the soft palate are not working effectively, so that the back of the soft palate is drooping down. The resonance is diverted from the mouth to the nasal cavities.

This can be corrected by appropriate exercises to strengthen the muscles which lift the soft palate. Gentle sucking, as on a straw, is one such exercise. ***(See The Essential Anatomy, Chapter 4, Modifying Sound - The Resonators, The Nose and Head Sinuses AND Training the Singing Voice, Chapter 4, What is Good Singing? The Voice Sounds Clear, Nasality – Soft Palate Exercise)***

Tension in the Jaw

When the muscles in the jaw are persistently contracted and tense, the jaw will appear stiff and articulation will be restricted. If there is tension in the jaw there will probably also be tension in the root of the tongue, neck and shoulders.

Muscles will release when stretched, so gentle exercise such as turning the head to the left, then back to the centre, then to the right and back to the centre, will ease tension. Neck and shoulder massage for chronic cases is advisable.

To help release the jaw, create a vacuum with the lower lip on the upper teeth and pull the jaw down vigorously. It's like making an "fff" sound, but sucking in rather than exhaling. The muscles being exercised by this action work in opposition to the muscles which clench the jaw. This helps to restore the balance of the two muscle groups. ***(See Training the Singing Voice, Chapter 4, What is Good Singing? The Voice Sounds Clear – The Tongue and Tension in the Jaw and Tongue)***

Tension in the Root of the Tongue

Tension in the root of the tongue can occur because there are several muscle groups at work, and sometimes they may be working in opposition. Muscles can lose the ability to relax, and so they remain contracted, which can interfere with the work of other muscles around them.

Tongue root tension can be eased by stretching the tongue. Poke it out to its full length and then release it. You can feel the root of the tongue being stretched. Tongue twisters such as "red lorry, yellow lolly", and tongue trills on an "rrr" are also useful in releasing tongue tension. ***(See Training the Singing Voice, Chapter 4, What is Good Singing? The Voice Sounds Clear – The Tongue and Tension in the Jaw and Tongue)***

Wrong Positioning of the Tongue

The tongue is a large organ and comprises several muscle groups. Because of its size, it can interfere with the rise and fall of the larynx, and even block the pharynx so that the sound is muffled.

If it sits too far back in the mouth and down in the throat, the larynx has trouble rising and high notes will be difficult to access. An habitual back position of the tongue may be the result of the native language or of the regional accent. Singers should be made aware of this and learn to control the position of the tongue to make their singing easier. ***(See Training the Singing Voice, Chapter 4, What is Good Singing? The Voice Sounds Clear – The Tongue and Tension in the Jaw and Tongue)***

In Conclusion

Recognising and remedying vocal difficulties depends on your knowledge of the essential anatomy of singing and your understanding of your student. No teacher can hope to solve all vocal problems in one go. Even simple ones take time to sort out. There are no quick fixes. Often, a vocal difficulty is the result of years of habit, and may be a combination of more than one of the above issues. Retraining the muscle memory into new habits takes time. You and your student need to work together to resolve them.

GLOSSARY OF TERMS

Glossary of Terms

Abdomen The lower part of the main body cavity, containing the stomach, intestines and other organs.

Abdominals The muscles in and around the abdomen.

Abduction/Abducted The moving of a body part away from the central axis. In this book, used in relation to the True Vocal Folds moving apart.

Adam's Apple A colloquial term referring to the hard lump at the front of the throat formed by the thyroid cartilage of the larynx.

Adduction/Adducted The moving/movement of a body part to the central axis. In this book, used in relation to the True Vocal Folds coming together in the centre.

Alignment The relationship between length of the spine and breadth across the chest.

Alveolar Ridge The hard ridge behind and above the upper teeth, housing the tooth sockets.

Anatomy The scientific study of the body and how its parts are arranged.

Articulators The articulators in speech and singing are the tongue, teeth and lips.

Aryepiglottic Sphincter The ring of muscle at the base of the epiglottis and situated at the top of the thyroid cartilage. The narrowing of this sphincter produces a voice quality known as 'squillo' or 'twang'.

Arytenoid Cartilages The horn-shaped structures which sit on the shoulders of the cricoid cartilage, and which control the vibrations of the true vocal folds.

Aural Relating to the ear, hearing and the response to all sound.

Baritone The baritone is the most common of male voices, and indicates a vocal colour more than a range. Many baritones can access both bass and tenor notes, but feel comfortable in the middle range of the voice. Again, there can be high, light, lyric and dramatic classifications of the baritone voice.

Bass The bass is the lowest of the male voices, with dark tone and especial strength at the bottom end of the range. They are not usually expected to sing high notes, but often can produce them easily. True basses, like true contraltos, are rare.

bel canto 18th-Century Italian singing style, with emphasis placed upon perfect technique and beauty of tone.

Bleat A fast, unpleasant vibrato arising from incorrect control of air flow.

Cardiovascular Relating to both the heart and blood vessels.

Cartilage A strong stretchy fibrous tissue which provides support to the skeleton. Cartilage can be soft, as in the ear lobe, and firm, as in the larynx.

"Chest" Voice The chest acts as a secondary resonator, and is responsive to lower pitches and a lower larynx. What is often referred to as a "chest" voice arises from the sensations of resonance in the chest cavity and lower throat, in response to lower pitches and thicker true vocal folds. It is not a separate "voice" at all.

Clavicle(s) or collarbone is a slender bone between the shoulder and neck, situated at the top of the rib-cage, on each side of the body.

Coloratura Literally, "coloured". It refers to the agility particularly demanded by Classical and Romantic period music across all voice types. Sometimes called "florid" music.

Consonant A speech sound or letter of the alphabet which is not a vowel. Consonants are pronounced by stopping the air from flowing freely through the mouth, especially by closing the lips or touching the teeth with the tongue.

Constriction/Constrict The action of the false vocal folds when they bear down upon the true vocal folds, with harmful effect. The opposite of constriction is retraction.

Contraction A bunching of a muscle caused by the shortening in length of the muscle fibres.

Contralto The lowest female voice is the contralto, which is dark and full in tone and lies comfortably in the lower register. Often the higher notes are limited in this type of voice. A true contralto voice is quite rare.

Counter-tenor The male voice which sings in the same general range as the lower female voices and is also called the male alto. This type of voice emerges after puberty, has a distinctive timbre which is unlike the female voices, and often sings a similar repertoire of early music as the mezzo-soprano voice. It is usually a form of developed falsetto.

Cricoid Cartilage The lowermost section of the larynx or voice box.

Diaphragm The wide sheet of muscle attached to the lower edges of the rib cage and to the spine, separating the chest cavity (thorax) from the abdominal cavity. The action of the diaphragm is to inflate and deflate the lungs with air.

Diction The clarity with which words are pronounced when speaking or singing.

Ensemble (from the French, "together") A group of two or more musicians performing together.

Epiglottis The thin lid-like flap of soft cartilage, suspended at the base of the tongue, which closes the opening to the larynx when food or drink is being swallowed.

Exhalation The process of breathing air out of the lungs.

False Vocal Folds Two bands of tissue which lie above the true vocal folds within the thyroid, and together with the true vocal folds, reinforce closure of the glottis, thus protecting the airways. Sometimes referred to as ventricular folds.

Forte An instruction in music to sing or play loudly.

Genre A classification or category which music can be divided into regarding style or form.

Glottis The space between the vocal folds, through which air passes.

Harmony Any combination of notes sung or played at the same time.

Haute-contre A male tenor voice, capable of singing in a very high tessitura.

"Head" Voice The head acts as a primary resonator, and is responsive to higher pitches and a raised larynx. This term refers to the sound arising from the higher pitches of a raised larynx with thinner vocal folds. The resonance is felt mainly in the head which accounts for the name. It is not a separate voice at all.

Holistic Dealing with or treating the whole of someone or something, not just one part.

Idiom The distinguishing artistic style of expression when applied to music in performance.

Inhalation The process of breathing air into the lungs.

Laryngo-Pharynx The space directly above the vocal folds; the bottom section of the Pharynx.

Laryngoscope A medical instrument consisting of a short metal or plastic tube fitted with a tiny light bulb, used when examining the larynx and the vocal folds in action.

Laryngeal Posture The way the component parts of the larynx relate to each other in voice qualities.

Larynx The valve constrictor situated at the top of the trachea (windpipe) through which air passes into and out of the lungs. Made up of the thyroid and cricoid cartilages and suspended from the hyoid bone, it is also responsible for all forms of voice production.

Legato Describes music which is to be sung or played in a smooth continuous way, often indicated in a music score by a curved line or slur. It is the opposite to staccato.

Ligament A ligament is a short band of tissue which connects bones to other bones to form a joint. A ligament is only slightly elastic and can be damaged if overstretched.

Lungs The two large spongy sacs situated within the rib cage where oxygen is extracted from the inhaled air, and carbon dioxide is extracted. Our means of breathing.

Male alto The male voice which sings in the same general range as the lower female voices and is also called the counter-tenor. This type of voice emerges after puberty, has a distinctive timbre which is unlike the female voices, and often sings a similar repertoire of early music as the mezzo-soprano voice. It is usually a form of developed falsetto.

Messa di voce A gradual crescendo and decrescendo on a sustained sung note.

Mezzo-soprano The mezzo-soprano voice may have the same range of notes as the soprano, but feels more comfortable singing in the middle and lower range of the voice. Often the sound is darker and warmer than the soprano, and can also fall into coloratura and dramatic categories.

Mime To pretend to sing, play or say something without making any sound.

Muscle The voluntary muscle tissue which we use for singing is composed of bundles of fibres which are capable of contracting and releasing to produce movement.

Nasality The sound produced when the soft palate is lowered, allowing any spoken or sung sound to resonate in the nasal cavity.

Naso-Pharynx The space behind the nose; the top of the Pharynx.

Navel The small hollow or scar at the point where the umbilical cord was attached.

Onset The start of a sound. There are several different types of onset. The most basic is the glottal, where the vocal folds are fully closed and opened by a puff of air as the sound is made. The next type is the aspirate, where the air flows over the folds and they then close to produce sound. The ideal onset for singing is where vocal fold closure occurs simultaneously with air flow.

Oro-Pharynx The space at the back of the mouth; the middle section of the Pharynx.

Passaggio This is a transition or passageway between two registers in the voice; the notes upon which the transition occurs.

Pharynx The throat or vocal tract, tube-like in shape, consisting of the naso-pharynx, oro-pharynx and laryngo-pharynx.

Piano An instruction in music to sing or play softly.

Pineal Gland A small cone-shaped organ of the brain that secretes the hormone melatonin into the bloodstream.

Portamento A smooth sliding between two pitches, primarily used in singing and string instruments.

Postlude A final or concluding phrase.

Posture Defined by the Spine

Pronunciation The way in which words are said or sung in any given language.

Psychology - scientific study of the human mind, mental state and resultant behaviour

Register The transition from one area of the voice to another (low to middle to high ranges) is called a register change. The notes upon which the register change occurs is called the "passaggio". Notes in the "passaggio" often feel weaker but should never be forced. If force is used moving from a lower to a higher register, the transition into the next register will not easily happen. The voice will sound driven and pushed.

Resonator A device for allowing sound to vibrate and continue. This is the pharynx (throat) in a singer or the hollow body of a violin for example.

Retraction/Retract The act of pulling something back or apart. In singing and speaking this refers to drawing the false vocal folds apart, and is the opposite of constriction.

Rhythm A regularly repeated pattern of beats, sounds, words or musical notes used in music, poetry and dancing.

Rib Cage The structure of ribs forming a protective bony enclosure surrounding the heart and lungs.

Sinus The sinuses are any of the spaces inside the head which are connected to the back of the nose. They can act as resonators.

Soft Palate The fleshy rear portion of the roof of the mouth, extending from the hard palate at the front and tapering to the hanging uvula at the rear. It elevates to close off the nasal passages when swallowing, sucking, and pronouncing certain sounds.

Soprano The soprano may be the highest of the female voices, but there are many different types of soprano. The lighter types of soprano have agility (coloratura) with a wide vocal range and ease at the top of the voice. These are categorised as light and lyric sopranos. The heavier, darker voices are called spinto and dramatic sopranos, but these also have good top notes.

Spine The line of vertebrae down the centre of the back which provides support for the body, protects the spinal cord and defines our posture.

Spinto From the Italian "spingere", to push. This denotes a heavier voice with a darker timbre, requiring a great breath support.

Staccato Describes music in which the notes are performed in a detached and separate way, with silences in between each note. It is the opposite to legato.

Sternum or breastbone, is the long, flat bone in the centre of the chest.

Style A distinctive and identifiable form within an artistic medium, such as Music, literature or architecture.

Tendon A strong band of tough fibrous tissue which connects muscle to bone.

Tenor The tenor is the high male voice which carries the middle voice sound up the scale into a upper register without changing to falsetto. There are as many subdivisions of tenor as there are for soprano: light, lyric, spinto, dramatic, and helden or heroic, all indicating differences in vocal weight and colour.

Tessitura This is where the voice sits most comfortably, irrespective of an ability to attain high or low notes; similarly with the range of a song.

Thick Folds This refers to the condition of the true vocal folds when a good deal of muscle mass is engaged. The sound is usually loud.

Thin Folds This refers to the condition of the true vocal folds when little muscle mass is engaged, and the fine edges of the folds approximate in adduction. The sound is usually soft; however, twang also employs thin vocal fold mass.

Thorax The area of the chest cavity.

Throat The pharynx and front part of the neck. It is the space down which food and air passes and houses the larynx.

Thyroid Cartilage The principal structure in the larynx forming the projection known as the Adam's Apple. It houses the vocal folds.

Timbre The quality or colour of tone of a voice or instrument as opposed to the pitch or volume.

Tongue The large muscle group located in the mouth used for tasting and articulating.

Torso The upper part of the body, not including the head and arms, and sometimes referred to as the trunk.

Trachea The wind-pipe or air tube extending from the larynx to the lungs which carries the flow of air.

True Vocal Folds The two folds of muscular tissue situated in the thyroid cartilage of the larynx which vibrate and produce sound when air is expelled from the lungs.

Unison The performance two or more parts at the same pitch or an octave apart.

Vibrato A slight variation in pitch resulting from the free vibration of the true vocal folds and movement of the larynx due to the air flow.

Vocal Ligament The edge of the true vocal folds, seen as a strong strip of white tissue on camera.

Vocal Tract The pharynx or throat. This is the airway used in the production of singing and speech; the passage above the larynx, including the pharynx, mouth and nasal cavities.

Voice Qualities Different types of sound, and directly related to the moving components of the larynx.

Vowel A speech sound produced when the breath flows out through the mouth without being blocked by the tongue, teeth or lips.

Windpipe The trachea or air tube extending from the larynx to the lungs which carries the flow of air.

Wobble A wobble in the voice is really a wide vibrato, caused by loss of breath support or too much air pressure. It may be remedied by correcting these and adding firmer neck anchoring.

APPENDIX I

APPENDIX II

Song Genres and Styles

The following lists are not exhaustive. They are included here as a guide to help you to explore songs of different periods, in order that you widen your range of repertoire.

Genre : the classification of types of song :

folk song
classical
musical theatre
jazz & blues
commercial pop
rock

Style : subdivisions of the classifications

Folk Song

traditional and national (English, French, Welsh etc)
Auprès de ma blonde (My Father's Garden)
The Miller of Dee,

neo (Peter Paul & Mary, Simon & Garfunkel)
If I Had a Hammer
Scarborough Fair

Classical

Early Music (before 9th Century)

Medieval or Gothic (9th to 14th centuries):

Guillaume de Machaut

Renaissance (15th and 16th centuries):

Caccini
Di Lasso
Dufay
Palestrina

Baroque (1600 - 1750):

Bach
Bononcini
Caldara
Giordani
Händel
Monteverdi
Pergolesi
Purcell
Scarlatti
Schutz

Classical (1750 - 1820):

early Beethoven
Gluck
Haydn
Mozart
Salieri

Romantic (1820 - 1910):

late Beethoven
Bellini
Bizet
Brahms
Donizetti
Dvorak
Fauré
Gounod
Grieg
Mahler
Mendelssohn
Puccini
Rossini
Schubert
Schumann
Tchaikovsky
Verdi
Wagner
Wolf

Modern (1910 - present):

Bartok
Britten
Butterworth
Debussy
Delius
Elgar
de Falla
Finzi
Gurney
Head
Holst
Ireland
Janacek
Parry
Poulenc
Prokofiev
Rachmaninov
Ravel
Rubbra
Richard Strauss
Shostakovich
Stanford
Tippett
Walton
Vaughan Williams
Williamson

Musical Theatre

Songs from Music Hall, such as:

Burlington Bertie
Down at the Old Bull and Bush
My Old Man Said Follow the Van
On Mother Kelly's Doorstep

Songs from Vaudeville, such as:

After The Ball
I Wonder Who's Kissing Her Now?
Let The Rest of the World Go By
Shine On Harvest Moon

Songs by Composers such as:

Adam Guettel
Alan Menken
Andrew Lippa
Andrew Lloyd Webber
Barry Manilow
Barry, Robin & Maurice Gibb
Benny Andersson/Bjorn Ulvaeus
Bob Merrill
Brenda Russell/Allee Willis/Stephen Bray
Brian Gari
Burt Bacharach
Burton Lane
Carol Hall
Charles Miller
Charles Strouse
Charlie Smalls
Claibe Richardson
Clark Gesner
Claude-Michel Schonberg
Cole Porter
Cy Coleman
Cyril Ornadel

Dan Goggin
Dana P Rowe
Danny Elfman
David Heneker
David Nield
David Shire
David Yazbek
DeSylva/Brown/Henderson
Dick Gallagher
Duke Ellington
Duncan Sheik
Edward Kleban
Elton John
Elvis Presley
Frank Churchill
Frank Lazarus
Frank Loesser
Frank Wildhorn
Frederick Loewe
Galt MacDermot
Gary Adler/Michael Patrick Walker
Gene de Paul
Geoff Stephens
George Gershwin
George Stiles
Glen Hansard
Harold Arlen
Harry Warren
Harvey Schmidt
Henry Krieger
Henry Mancini
Howard Goodall
Irving Berlin
Ivor Novello
Jacques Brel
Janet Hood
Jason Howland
Jason Robert Brown
Jeanine Tesori
Jeff Bowen
Jelly Roll Morton
Jerome Kern
Jerry Bock

Jerry Herman
Jerry Lieber/Mike Stoller
Jim Jacobs/Warren Casey
Jim Wise
Jimmy Roberts
John Barry
John Du Prez & Eric Idle
John Kander
John Taylor/David Heneker
Jonathan Larson
Jule Styne
Julian Slade
Keith Herrmann
Kurt Weill
Larry Grossman
Laurence O'Keefe & Nell Benjamin
Leonard Bernstein
Leslie Bricusse
Lin-Manuel Miranda
Lionel Bart
Lisa Lambert & Greg Morrison
Lucy Simon
Madness
Marc Shaiman
Mark Hollmann
Mark Schoenfeld/Barri McPherson
Marvin Hamlisch
Mary Murfitt
Mary Rodgers
Matthew Sklar
Maury Yeston
Mel Brooks
Meredith Wilson
Michael Gore
Michael John LaChiusa
Michel Legrand
Millard & Finch
Mitch Leigh
Nancy Ford
Noel Coward
Noel Gay
Parker, Lopez & Stone
Paul Gordon

Paul McKibbins
Peter Allen
Phil Collins
Queen
Richard Adler
Richard Cocciante
Richard M. Sherman/Robert B. Sherman
Richard O'Brien
Richard Rodgers
Richard Thomas
Ricky Ian Gordon
Robert Lopez/Jeff Marx
Robert Nassif-Lindsey
Robert Waldman
Robert Wright
Robert Wright/George Forrest
Ron Grainer
Rupert Holmes
Sammy Fain
Sandy Wilson
Scott Frankel
Sherman Edwards
Stephen Flaherty
Stephen Schwartz
Stephen Sondheim
Stephen Trask
Steve Dorff
Steve Margoshes
Steve Schalchlin
Stew
Tim Minchin
Tom Kitt
Tom Snow
Tony Hatch/Jackie Trent
Vincent Youmans
Vivian Ellis
William Finn
William May
Willy Russell

Songs from Shows, such as:

Title	**Show Dates**
Utopia Ltd	1893
The Enchantress	1911
Stop! Look! Listen!	1915
A To Z	1921
No, No Nanette	1925
Metropolis	1927
Show Boat	1927
Connecticut Yankee	1927
The New Moon	1928
Private Lives	1930
The New Yorkers	1930
Americana	1932
Roberta	1933
Keeps Rainin' All The Time	1933
Nymph Errant	1933
Born To Dance	1934
Glamorous Nights	1935
Porgy and Bess	1935
Top Hat	1935
Careless Rapture	1936
Swing Time (film)	1936
Damsel in Distress	1937
Me & My Girl	1937
My One And Only	1937
Boys From Syracuse	1938
The Dancing Years	1939
The Wizard of Oz	1939
Lady in the Dark	1941
Carmen Jones	1943
Hello, Frisco, Hello (Film)	1943
Something For The Boys	1943
One Touch of Venus	1943
Oklahoma	1943
On The Town	1944
The Firebrand of Florence	1945
Carousel	1945
Annie get your Gun	1946
Finnian's Rainbow	1946

Title	Show Dates
Easter Parade	1947
Street Scene	1947
Brigadoon	1947
Kiss me Kate	1948
Kink's Rhapsody	1949
South Pacific	1949
Guys and Dolls	1950
Lost in the Stars	1950
Out of This World	1950
The King & I	1951
Zip Goes A Million	1951
The Pajama Game	1952
Calamity Jane	1953
Kismet	1953
Tom Lehrer	1953
Wonderful Town	1953
Salad Days	1954
Candide	1955
Damn Yankees	1955
Guys & Dolls	1955
High Society	1955
Shoestring Revue	1955
State Fair	1955
Sugar Babies	1955
Bells Are Ringing	1956
The Most Happy Fella	1956
West Side Story	1956
My Fair Lady	1956
The Music Man	1957
Cinderella	1957
Flower Drum Song	1958
An Evening Wasted With Tom Lehrer	1958
Nunsense	1958
The Sound of Music	1959
Gypsy	1959
Babes in Arms	1959
Jacques Brel is Alive & Well	1959
Once upon a Mattress	1959
Do Re Mi	1960
The Fantasticks	1960

Title	Show Dates
Bye Bye Birdie	1960
Camelot	1960
Oliver	1960
Carnival	1961
And The World Goes Round	1961
Stop The World - I Want To Get Off	1961
A Funny Thing Happened On The Way to the Forum	1962
Little Me	1962
Half a Sixpence	1963
Hello Dolly	1963
One Hundred & Ten in The Shade	1963
She Loves Me	1963
Anyone Can Whistle	1964
Fiddler On The Roof	1964
Robert and Elizabeth	1964
Funny Girl	1964
Seventeen Seventy Six (1776)	1964
Flora, The Red Menace	1965
The Likes of Us	1965
Charlie Girl	1965
Man of La Mancha	1965
The Roar of The Greasepaint, The Smell of the Crowd	1965
Sweet Charity	1965
Do I Hear A Waltz?	1965
On A Clear Day You Can See Forever	1965
You're a Good Man, Charlie Brown	1965
The Apple Tree	1966
Mame	1966
Cabaret	1966
Evening Primrose	1966
Hair	1966
The Life	1966
Doctor Dolittle	1967
Once Upon A Mattress	1967
Joseph and the Amazing Technicolor Dreamcoat	1968
Promises, Promises	1968
Zorba	1968

Title	Show Dates
Return To The Forbidden Planet	1968
Hair	1968
Dear World	1968
Minnie's Boys	1969
Jesus Christ Superstar	1970
Company	1970
Godspell	1971
Follies	1971
Seesaw	1972
Pippin	1972
Chicago	1973
The Card	1973
Mack & Mabel	1974
The Wiz	1974
Jeeves	1975
A Chorus Line	1975
Snoopy	1975
Funny Lady	1975
Nine	1975
Evita	1976
Bugsy Malone	1976
Starting Here, Starting Now	1976
I'm Getting My Act Together and Taking It on the Road	1976
Rock Nativity	1976
The Baker's Wife	1977
New York, New York	1977
Saturday Night Fever	1977
The Act	1978
On The 20th Century	1978
Ballroom	1978
The Best Little Whorehouse In Texas	1978
Working	1978
Tell Me On A Sunday	1979
Fame - The Film	1979
Sweeney Todd	1979
They're Playing Our Song	1979
The Biograph Girl	1980
Barnum	1980
Cats	1981

Title	**Show Dates**
Victor/Victoria	1981
Falsettos	1981
Merrily We Roll Along	1981
Woman of The Year	1981
Tin Pan Ali	1981
Song and Dance	1982
Little Shop of Horrors	1982
Baby	1983
Blood Brothers	1983
Dance A Little Closer	1983
Is There Life After High School?	1983
La Cage Aux Folles	1983
Yentl	1983
Starlight Express	1984
Chess	1984
Footloose	1984
Saturday Night	1984
The Hired Man	1984
Sunday In The Park With George	1984
Just So!	1984
Les Miserables	1985
Cricket	1986
The Phantom of the Opera	1986
The Mystery of Edwin Drood	1986
Rags	1986
Into The Woods	1988
Romance Romance	1988
Aspects of Love	1989
City of Angels	1989
Grand Hotel	1989
Closer Than Ever	1989
Miss Saigon	1989
Kiss of The Spider Woman	1989
A Slice Of Saturday Night	1989
Once on this Island	1990
Jekyll & Hyde	1990
Dick Tracey: The Motion Picture	1990
Napoleon	1990
Children of Eden	1991
Beauty & The Beast	1991

Title	Show Dates
My Favorite Year	1991
Diamonds	1991
The Will Rogers Follies	1991
The Secret Garden	1991
Sunset Boulevard	1991
Weird Romance	1992
The Scarlet Pimpernel	1992
Balancing Act	1992
Nick & Nora	1992
Eating Raoul	1992
Newsies	1992
Aladdin	1993
Elegies	1993
The Goodbye Girl	1993
Sunset Boulevard	1993
My Favourite Year	1993
Nightmare Before Christmas	1993
Copacabana	1994
The Lion King	1994
Kicks	1994
Lucky Stiff	1994
Passion	1994
Lunch	1994
Side Show	1994
Pocahontas	1995
Rent	1995
Whoop Dee Doo!	1995
Whistle Down the Wind	1996
Always	1996
Big	1996
Frame By Frame	1996
I Love You, You're Perfect, Now Change	1996
Fame - The Musical	1996
Hunchback of Notre Dame	1996
The Life	1996
Martin Guerre 1	1996
Ragtime	1996
Titanic	1996
Songs For A New World	1996

Title	Show Dates
The Fix	1997
Honk	1997
Hercules	1997
King David	1997
Steel Pier	1997
Bat Boy	1997
The Civil War	1998
Aida	1998
Footloose	1998
New Brain, A	1998
Parade	1998
The Boy from OZ	1998
Martin Guerre 2	1998
Parade	1998
The Scarlet Pimpernel 2	1998
Wearing Someone Else's Clothes	1998
Myths & Hymns	1998
The Wild Party	1999
The Beautiful Game	2000
The Full Monty	2000
Jane Eyre	2000
Geppetto	2000
Notre Dame de Paris	2000
The Witches of Eastwick	2000
Hairspray	2001
Seussical	2001
Thoroughly Modern Millie	2001
Moulin Rouge	2001
The Last 5 Years	2002
Sweet Smell of Success	2002
A Man of No Importance	2002
The IT Girl	2002
Taboo	2002
Avenue Q	2003
Wicked	2003
John and Jen	2003
Little Women	2004
Woman in White	2004
Spamalot - Monty Python's	2005
Tarzan	2006

Title	Show Dates
Sister Act	2006
Shrek	2008
13 The Musical	2008
Unauthorised Autobiography of Samantha Brown	2009
Catch Me If You Can	2009
Next To Normal	2009
Love Never Dies	2010
Book of Mormon, The	2011
Stephen Ward the Musical	2013
Dogfight	2013
School of Rock	2015

Jazz & Blues

Songs by Artistes such as:

Billie Holliday
Duke Ellington
Nat King Cole
Bessie Smith
Louis Armstrong
Sarah Vaughan
Ella Fitzgerald
Cleo Laine

Commercial Pop

Songs by Artistes such as:

Bing Crosby
Frank Sinatra
Dionne Warwick George
Benson
Billy Joel
Madonna
ABBA
The Carpenters
Matt Munroe
Doris Day
Neil Diamond
John Denver
George Michael
Cliff Richard
Boyzone
Spandau Ballet
Duran Duran
Take That
Simon and Garfunkel Billy
Joel
Tom Jones
Carole King
Whitney Houston Maria
Carey
Barry Manilow
Bette Midler
Céline Dion

REM
Barbra Streisand
Carly Simon
Dionne Warwick
Diana Ross
Robbie Williams
Will Young
Olly Murs
Britney Spears
Taylor Swift
Tom Odell
Adele
Rhianna
Beyoncé
Girls Aloud
Spice Girls
Amy Winehouse
Norah Jones
Alicia Keys
The Shires
KT Tunstall
Mumford & Sons

Rock

Songs by Artistes such as:

Elvis Presley
Dusty Springfield
The Beatles
Bryan Adams
Avril Lavigne
Elton John
Bon Jovi
Queen (Freddy Mercury)
Oasis
Blur
Radiohead
Nikelback
The Foo Fighters
AC-DC
Iron Maiden
ZZ Top

Metallica
Deep Purple
The Eagles
Pink Floyd
Aerosmith
Nirvana
Linkin Park
My Chemical Romance
Fun Loving Criminals
Red Hot Chilli Peppers
Green Day
The Gaslight Anthem
Eric Clapton
Counting Crows
Meatloaf
U2
Bruce Springstein
The Killers
Kings Of Leon
Paramore

Appendix II
Image Referencing

Fig 1.
Overall View of the Anatomy of Singing - Page 18
License Info: Image purchased, and used under Adobe Stock Standard License conditions. Variations of this image on pages 18, 26 & 30 are also used under Adobe Stock Standard License conditions. Adobe ID #92097978 for further information, please visit www.stock.adobe.com

Fig 2.
The Actions of the Diaphragm - Page 31
This image is used under the Creative Commons License 4.0.
Originator: OpenStax College http://cnx.org/contact/col11496/1.6/
Minor alteration: addition of "Diaphragm', and line in Diagram B.

Fig 3. The Location Of The Larynx - Page 34
License Info: Image purchased, and used under Adobe Stock Standard License conditions. Adobe ID #75458952 for further information, please visit www.stock.adobe.com

Fig 4. The Thyroid Cartilage - Page 36
Image Used under the Creative Commons License 3.0
Originator: https://bioass.wikispaces.com
human+larynx+and+the+production+of+sound
https://creativecommons.org/licenses/by-sa/3.0/

Fig 8. The Arytenoid Cartilages Opening and Closing the Glottis - Page 38
License Info: Image purchased, and used under Adobe Stock Standard License conditions. Adobe ID #63814088 for further information, please visit www.stock.adobe.com

Fig 11. "Diagram of the Vocal Chords Seen From Above," - Page 42
Image Reproduced under Public Domain License.
https://commons.wikimedia.org/wiki/File:Larynx_(top_view).jpg
Modified by Novordium.

Fig 12. "The False Vocal Folds," - Page 43
Image Modified from an original source in the Public Domain
https://commons.wikimedia.org/wiki/File:Illu_larynx.jpg
This image ©Novordium 2016

Fig 14. "The Resonators" - Page 47
Image used under Public Domain License granted by original illustrator Alan Hoofring
https://commonswikimedia.org/wiki/File Larynx_and_nearby_structures.jpg

Figs "5,6,7,9,10,13,15,16,17" Various: - Pages: 37,38,39,40,44,58,62,83
Illustrations of The Larynx in various tilt positions:
All B&W pictures/illustrations of "the Larynx," in various positions, Image(s) by Oliver Boito please visit www.oliverboito.com for more of his work ©Novordium 2016

Cover Image: Purchased, modified and reproduced under iStock.com Standard License Parameters image ref 452690849

Section 1 Image: Sourced and reproduced under Creative Commons License Absfreepic.com ref 20985.

Section 2 Image: From Authors Personal Library © Ross Campbell 2017.

Section 3 Image: From Authors Personal Library © Ross Campbell 2017.

Section 4 Image: Purchased and reproduced under Adobe Stock Standard License Image ID ref #21858412.

Section 5 Image: Sourced and reproduced under Creative Commons License Pixabay.com ref 4997826.

Section 6 Image: Sourced and reproduced under Creative Commons License Pixabay.com ref 522604.

Section 7 Image: Sourced and reproduced under Creative Commons License Absfreepic.com ref 67109.

Section 8 Image: Sourced and reproduced under Creative Commons License Pixabay.com ref 499311.

Section 9 Image: Sourced and reproduced from Unsplash.com. Credit for image Cole Keister.

Section 10 Image: Sourced and reproduced under Creative Commons License Pixabay.com ref 466950.

Glossary Image: Sourced and reproduced from Unsplash.com. Credit for image Dmitrij Paskevic.

Lightning Source UK Ltd.
Milton Keynes UK
UKHW05n1643010518
321939UK00005B/36/P